Problem Solving Workbook

with Reading Strategies

TEACHER'S EDITION
Grade 5

Harcourt Brace & Company

Orlando • Atlanta • Austin • Boston • San Francisco • Chicago • Dallas • New York • Toronto • London

http://www.hbschool.com

ISBN 0-15-311111-9

5 6 7 8 9 10 054 2000

CONTENTS

Using Numbers

Write the correct answer.

1. Write *cardinal*, *ordinal*, or *nominal* to describe the 5 in "I am 5 feet 4 inches tall."

   _____**cardinal**_____

2. Write *cardinal*, *ordinal*, or *nominal* to describe the numbers in, "My phone number is 555-1234."

   _____**nominal**_____

3. Tell which number in the headline is an ordinal number.

   McCoy Finishes 2nd in the 1999 5-Mile Fun-Run

   _____**2nd**_____

4. Tell which number in the headline is a cardinal number.

   Ruiz Finishes 1st in the 5-Kilometer Run

   _____**5**_____

Choose the letter of the correct answer.

5. Which of these numbers is a nominal number?

   A 2 in. border   **B** 2nd place
   C 162 Oak Street   **D** 2 sisters

6. Tad buys a pinwheel for $0.79 and gives the cashier a $1 bill. How much change should he get back?

   F $0.21   **G** $2.10
   H $0.79   **J** $0.10

7. The Breugers go to the furniture store to buy a kitchen table and six chairs. The table costs $99. What other information do the Breugers need before they can calculate the total cost for their kitchen set?

   A How many chairs they will buy
   B The cost of one table
   C The cost of one chair
   D How much their old table cost
   E How much profit the store will make

8. The tongue twister below has more than one kind of number. Which kinds of numbers does it have?

   "The sixth sick shepherd has six sick sheep in six six-sided shacks."

   F Cardinal and ordinal
   G Cardinal, ordinal, and nominal
   H Cardinal and nominal
   J Nominal and ordinal
   K Not Here

9. **Write About It** Explain how you decided which number in Problem 5 is a nominal number.

   Possible answer: A nominal number names something. 162 Oak Street
   names an address.

Benchmark Numbers

Write the correct answer.

1. Barbara packs 15 muffins in each box. Tuesday morning she delivers 40 boxes of muffins. Does Barbara deliver more than 300 muffins Tuesday morning?

_____ **yes** _____

2. Each section of the stadium holds about 100 people. There are 10 sections in the stadium. About how many people does the stadium hold?

_____ **about 1,000 people** _____

3. Is the number a *cardinal*, *ordinal*, or *nominal* number?

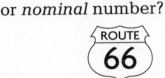

_____ **ordinal** _____

4. Is the number a *cardinal*, *ordinal*, or *nominal* number?

_____ **nominal** _____

Choose the letter of the correct answer.

5. Which estimate is most reasonable?
   - 25 students in a classroom
   - 12 classrooms in the school
   - About how many students in the school?

   A 120   **(B)** 250   **C** 2,500   **D** 34

6. Which estimate is most reasonable?
   - 8 cereal boxes in one case
   - 62 cases of cereal on the truck
   - About how many cereal boxes on the truck?

   F 70   **G** 300   **(H)** 500   **J** 5,000

7. A driver loads 300 cases of eggs on her empty truck. She delivers 120 cases and then 70 cases more. She then loads another 100 cases. Which expression shows the total number of cases on the truck?

   A 300 + 120 + 70 + 100
   B 300 − 120 + 70 − 100
   (C) 300 − 120 − 70 + 100
   D 300 − 120 − 70 − 100

8. Ann Arbor, Michigan gets 36 in. of snow in December, 47 in. in January, 51 in. in February, and 32 in. in March. Which is the most reasonable estimate for the total amount of snow for the four months?

   F 1,200 in.   **G** 110 in.
   H 280 in.   **(J)** 170 in.
   K 3 ft

9. **Write About It** Explain how you chose the most reasonable estimate in Problem 8.

   Possible answer: I rounded each month's snowfall to the nearest ten and

   then added.

Place Value to Hundred Thousands

Write the correct answer.

1. In 1990, the population of Des Moines, Iowa, was 193,187. Write the value of the digit 3 in this number.

___3,000, or 3 thousands___

2. Write *cardinal*, *ordinal*, or *nominal* for the number.

Jeremy's phone number is 555–6780.

___nominal___

3. Edna has made a string of paper clips. When she put 20 clips together, her string was about 1 yd long. Her string now has 200 paper clips. Is it more than 5 yd long?

___yes___

4. Light travels about 186,000 miles in 1 second. Light from the Sun takes about 8 minutes to reach Earth. Which of these numbers has an 8 in the ten-thousands place?

___186,000___

Choose the letter of the correct answer.

5. Which is the value of the underlined digit?

342,4<u>4</u>8

A 4 **B** 40 **C** 400
D 4,000 **E** 40,000

6. Which is the standard form for 400,000 + 3,000 + 600 + 3?

F 40,363 **G** 4,363
H 400,363 **J** 403,603
K Not Here

7. The odometer on Carol's bike shows that she has biked 2 miles to the nearest $\frac{1}{10}$ mile. A mile is 5,280 feet. Which is the most reasonable estimate for the distance Carol biked in feet?

A 500 ft
B 10,000 ft
C 100,000 ft
D 500,000 ft

8. Jeb does 8 sets of 9 push-ups. Then he does another set of 11 push-ups. Which two operations would you use to find the total number of push-ups Jeb does?

F Addition and subtraction
G Multiplication and division
H Multiplication and addition
J Division and subtraction

9. Write About It Explain how you chose your answer to Problem 5.

___Possible answer: The underlined digit is 4 and it is in the tens place.___

___So, multiply 4 × 10 = 40.___

Place Value of Larger Numbers

Write the correct answer.

1. Write the value of the underlined digit in the following number.

   8,765,013,542

   8,000,000,000, or 8 billion

2. Write the following number in standard form.

   200,000 + 40,000 + 6,000 + 40 + 3

   246,043

3. The average distance between the Earth and the Sun is about 150,000,000 km. Write the value of the digit 1 in this number.

   100,000,000, or 1 hundred million

4. Scientists received a radio message from a satellite orbiting at about 430,000,000 km from Earth. Write this number in word form.

   four hundred thirty million

Choose the letter of the correct answer.

5. Which estimate is most reasonable?
   - 20 insects in each display case
   - 13 display cases in the museum
   - About how many insects in the museum?

   A 20   **B** 250   **C** 600
   D 2   **E** Not Here

6. Which of these is the value of the underlined digit?

   1<u>5</u>0,095,245,000

   F 5   **G** 5,000
   H 50,000,000   **J** 500,000,000
   K 50,000,000,000

7. Tyrone and Cal are playing a high-finance game in which they write each other play checks. Cal has written Tyrone checks for the amounts below. Which one is for $297,360,400?

   A two hundred ninety-seven thousand, three hundred sixty-four
   B twenty-nine million, seven hundred thirty-six thousand, four hundred
   C two hundred ninety-seven thousand, three hundred sixty, four hundred
   D two hundred ninety-seven million, three hundred sixty thousand, four hundred

8. Bigger Burger advertises it has sold 30,000,000 burgers. Burger Bagger claims it has sold twenty million burgers. About how many burgers have the two fast-food restaurants sold altogether?

   F 320,000,000 burgers
   G fifty thousand burgers
   H 50,000,000 burgers
   J two hundred thirty million burgers

9. **Write About It** In Problem 8, explain how you went about estimating the total.

   Possible answer: I wrote twenty

   million as 20,000,000, and then I

   added 20 + 30 to get 50,000,000.

Comparing and Ordering

Write the correct answer.

1. Which is greater, 58,820 *or* 58,280?

_____58,820_____

2. Write the word form for the value of the digit 7 in the number below.
97,000,999

_____seven million_____

3. Nettie's car goes about 30 miles on a gallon of gas. The gas tank holds 12 gallons. Which is a more reasonable estimate for the number of miles Nettie can drive on one tank of gas: 300 miles or 750 miles?

_____300 mi_____

4. The tri-city area has three towns. Scrayville has 28,302 people, Burton has 22,938 people, and Chatters has 31,011 people. Order the towns from greatest population to least.

_____Chatters, Scrayville, Burton_____

Choose the letter of the correct answer.

5. Which of these numbers has the least value?

(A) 98,898   **B** 98,988
C 98,989   **D** 98,899

6. Which is the greatest number?

F 45,729   **G** 54,729
(H) 54,927   **J** 45,972

7. Players A, B, C, D, and E all played a game. The highest scorer won. Their scores are below. Which player won?

(A) 32,094
B 28,927
C 31,375
D 32,049
E 23,940

8. Which of the numbers below is 3,000,000 more than 30,000,000?

F 30,030,000
G 60,000,000
H 30,300,000
J 30,003,000
(K) Not Here

9. Write About It In Problem 3, look at the number you did *not* choose for your answer. Explain why that number is not a reasonable estimate.

<u>**Possible answer: The total number of miles Nettie can go is 30 miles × 12**</u>

<u>**gallons of gas. Round 12 to 10: 30 × 10 = 300, so 750 is not a reasonable**</u>

<u>**estimate.**</u>

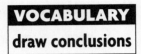

Drawing Conclusions

To solve a problem you may have to **draw conclusions** based on two or more ideas or pieces of information. Sometimes the information you need is in a table. Read the following problem.

VOCABULARY
draw conclusions

Jaime wants to write a report about a planet that has at least 2 moons and is more than 1,000 million miles away from the sun. Jaime will choose from the planets listed on the table. Which planet will he choose?

Planet	Number of Moons	Distance from Sun (in Millions of Miles)	Time to Revolve Around Sun
Neptune	8	2,800	165 years
Jupiter	16	480	12 years
Earth	1	93	1 year
Pluto	1	3,600	248 years

---

1. Look in the table under *Number of Moons* and *Distance from Sun*. Draw conclusions to solve the problem.

   The planets that have at least 2 moons are Neptune and Jupiter. Jupiter is

   only 480 million mi from the sun. Neptune is 2,800 million mi from the sun.

   Jamie will write a report on Neptune.

2. Describe the problem-solving strategy you used.

   Possible answer: I used a table to solve the problem.

Underline information you can use to draw conclusions about the problem. Solve.

3. The table above shows <u>how long it takes several planets to revolve around the sun</u> and their number of moons. <u>Which of the planets takes the most time? The least time?</u>

   Pluto; Earth

4. <u>Does the time it takes for a planet to revolve around the sun depend on its distance from the sun or on the number of moons it has?</u> Use the table to draw your conclusions.

   On its distance from the sun

Adding and Subtracting with Data

Write the correct answer.

1. Write a related subtraction sentence.

$$38 + 44 = 82$$

__82 − 44 = 38 or 82 − 38 = 44__

2. Write 329,280,300 in word form.

____three hundred twenty-nine____

____million, two hundred eighty____

____thousand, three hundred____

3. How many more cars did Elroy sell in 1997 than in 1998?

ELROY'S CAR SALES

Year	1995	1996	1997	1998
Cars Sold	64	51	92	68

_____24_____

4. Use the table from Problem 3. Write the number of cars Elroy sold each year in order from the least to the greatest.

____51, 64, 68, 92____

Choose the letter of the correct answer.

5. Which of the buttons below shows a *nominal* number?

A 3rd place
B 5th Grade Rocks!
C 101 Dalmatians
(D) Call 711

6. Juli played on the softball team for four years. Which number shows the total runs-batted-in she made during those four years?

Juli's Runs-Batted-In Record				
Year	1995	1996	1997	1998
Runs-batted-in	55	86	97	92

A 340   (B) 330   C 92
D 350   E Not Here

7. Which number sentence shows the inverse operation for the number sentence 38 + n = 77?

F $38 + 77 = n$ (G) $77 − 38 = n$
H $n + 38 = 77$ J $38 − n = 77$

8. Write About It Explain how you chose the correct answer in Problem 6.

__Possible answer: I used the table__

__to get the data for each year.__

__Then I added, because the__

__question asks for the total__

__runs-batted-in; the sum is 330__

__runs-batted-in.__

Subtracting Across Zeros

Write the correct answer.

1. Write the difference.

$$\begin{array}{r} 500 \\ -\ 236 \\ \hline \underline{264} \end{array}$$

2. Write a related addition sentence.

$$195 - 158 = 37$$

$$\underline{158 + 37 = 195,\ or\ 37 + 158 = 195}$$

3. Vera gets a $30,000 commission to make a sculpture for the museum. She spends $6,220 on materials. How much of the money is left?

_____ $23,780 _____

4. Four mountains in a range have these heights: Mt. Cobb: 3,259 ft; Mt. Noir: 3,522 ft; Mt. Tabor: 3,092 ft; Mt. Thunder: 2,948 ft. Order the mountains from the lowest to the highest.

Thunder, Tabor, Cobb, Noir

Choose the letter of the correct answer.

5. What is the value of the digit 3 in 9,397?

- **A** 3
- **B** 30
- **(C)** 300
- **D** 3,000

6. $7,100 - 3905 = \underline{\ ?\ }$

- **F** 4,295
- **G** 3,295
- **(H)** 3,195
- **J** 3,095

7. A school had 7,000 tickets to sell for a football game. They sold 5,300 of the tickets to students and 420 to faculty. How many tickets does the school have left?

- **A** 1,700 tickets
- **B** 2,120 tickets
- **C** 1,380 tickets
- **(D)** 1,280 tickets
- **E** Not Here

8. Theo wants to enter the number 3,295 into his calculator. By mistake, he enters 33,295. How can he get the correct number on the calculator display?

- **F** By subtracting 33,000
- **(G)** By subtracting 30,000
- **H** By subtracting 29,000
- **J** By subtracting 3,000
- **K** Not Here

9. Write About It Explain two different ways to solve Problem 7.

Possible answers: 1. Subtract 7,000 − 5,300 to get 1,700; then subtract

1,700 − 420 to get 1,280; 2. Add 5,300 + 420 to get 5,720; then subtract

7,000 − 5,720 to get 1,280.

Name _____

Choosing Addition or Subtraction

Write the correct answer.

1. Write the difference.

34,000
− 5,877

28,123

2. Order these numbers from least to greatest: 76,384; 23,658; 78,220; 76,800.

23,658; 76,384; 76,800; 78,220

3. Joan earns a score of 8,110 in round 1 of a video game. In round 2, she earns 7,090 points. How many points does she earn for the two rounds?

15,200 points

4. In Problem 3, how many more points did Joan score in round 1 than in round 2?

1,020 more points

Choose the letter of the correct answer.

5. Andrea is pricing two cars. The Neptune costs $9,999. The Satellite costs $9,299. Which expression can Andrea use to find how much more the Neptune costs?

A $9,999 + $9,299
(B) $9,999 − $9,299
C $9,299 × $9,999
D $9,299 ÷ $9,999

6. Water boils at 212°F. It freezes at 32°F. Room temperature is about 68°F. Which expression shows the difference between water's freezing and boiling points?

A 212 + 32
B 212 − 68
C 68 − 32
(D) 212 − 32

7. Jayne has $34 when she gets home from the store. She spent $18 at the store. How much money did she have when she went to the store?

(F) $52   G $34   H $18   J $16

8. Which of these problems would you use addition to solve?

F Lester weighed 281 lb. He lost 47 lb. What is his new weight?
G Bill grew 4 in. and is now 66 in. tall. How tall was he before?
(H) Jorge weighed 109 lb and gained 22 lb. What is his new weight?
J Verne is now 55 in. tall. Last year he was 49 in. tall. How much did he grow?
K Not Here

9. Write About It For Problem 3, explain how you chose an operation to use.

Possible answer: Problem 3 asks you to join groups, which requires

addition.

Estimation and Column Addition

Write the correct answer.

1. Estimate the sum.

```
   382
   512
   198
 + 342
```

Possible estimate: 1,400

2. Estimate the sum.

```
    32
    66
    57
 +  44
```

Possible estimate: 200

3. There were 476 tickets sold for a play. There were 800 tickets available. How many tickets were not sold?

324 tickets

4. In 1980, 388,291 people lived in the city of Sharpton. In 1990, 388,246 people lived in Sharpton. Did the number of people living in Sharpton increase or decrease?

It decreased.

Choose the letter of the correct answer.

5. Which is the most reasonable estimate of the sum?

```
   811
   382
   577
 + 683
```

A about 2,200   B about 2,300
(C) about 2,500   D about 2,800

6. Which number is the difference of 4,000 − 2,674?

F 2,326
G 1,426
H 2,226
(J) 1,326

7. Temin adds memory to his computer. First he adds 32 megabytes of memory. Then he adds 64 megabytes. This makes a total of 128 megabytes. How much memory was in the computer to start with?

A 16 megabytes (B) 32 megabytes
C 64 megabytes   D 28 megabytes
E 204 megabytes

8. Elena drove her new car 46,000 miles before getting it tuned up. The owner's manual says she should have the car tuned up every 30,000 miles. How many extra miles did she drive before getting the car tuned up?

F 30,000 mi   G 46,000 mi
H 60,000 mi   J 14,000 mi
(K) Not Here

9. **Write About It** Explain how you chose the most reasonable estimate in Problem 5.

Possible answer: I rounded each addend to the nearest hundred and then added the hundreds.

Using Context Clues

Context clues are the words or phrases that help you understand the meaning of a word, sentence, or paragraph. Read the following problem.

> Julia has $30.00 to spend at the party store. She spends $16.84 on party favors and $4.32 on decorations. Then she buys balloons for $2.55. About how much does Julia spend in all? What will be the exact total at the cash register?

1. Underline the context clues to help you decide whether you need to give an exact answer or an estimated answer to each question in the problem above. Then explain what the context clues tell you. **Possible answers given.**

Context Clues	**Explanation**
<u>About how much</u> does Julia spend in all?	**"About" means an estimate of the total; explanations will vary.**
<u>What will be the exact total</u> at the cash register?	**"Exact" means the actual total.**

2. Solve the problems.

   $16.84→$17.00; $4.32→$4.00; $2.55→$3.00; so Julia spends about $24.

   She pays $23.71 at the cash register.

3. Describe the strategy you used.

   Possible answer: I rounded to estimate the first answer; I added to find the

   second answer.

Underline the context clues. Solve the problem.

4. The class has $40.00 in its treasury. They give $15.85 to the Animal Rescue House and spend $11.37 for a basketball. <u>Will they be able to spend $30.00 on a class trip?</u>

   No, they would need about $57.00.

5. Max earns $20.00 mowing lawns. He wants to buy a CD for $10.50, a T-shirt for $3.78, and a book for $4.16. <u>Does he have enough money</u> to buy all 3 items? <u>How much money would he have to pay?</u>

   Yes, he needs about $19.00.

   He would pay $18.44.

Using Tenths and Hundredths

Write the correct answer.

1. Write the decimal for the model.

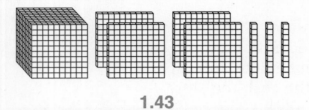

_____ 1.43 _____

2. Veronica earned $600 over the summer. She used $339 to buy a bike. How much money did she have left after she bought the bike?

_____ $261 _____

3. Write the decimal for the number, seven and nineteen hundredths.

_____ 7.19 _____

4. Four buses brought visitors to a park. The first bus held 38 people. The second held 46 people. The third held 51 people. The fourth held 39 people. About how many people were on the four buses?

_____ about 180 people _____

Choose the letter of the correct answer.

5. Tim and Jenny are buying two items. Tim estimates the total cost as $3,700. Jenny estimates the total cost as $4,000. One of the items costs $879. Which item below could be the second item?

A A $1,312 item
(B) A $2,821 item
C A $3,840 item
D A $3,300 item
E A $3,745 item

6. Pat, Cheryl, and Roy each have a pet. Pat doesn't like birds. Roy is allergic to cats. Cheryl is afraid of snakes. Which arrangement below is reasonable?

F Pat: snake; Cheryl: bird; Roy: cat
(G) Pat: cat; Cheryl: bird; Roy: snake
H Pat: bird; Cheryl: cat; Roy: snake
J Pat: cat; Cheryl: snake; Roy: bird
K Not Here

7. Which decimal does the model show?

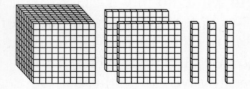

A 1.023
B 12.3
C 0.123
(D) 1.23

8. **Write About It** Explain how you chose your answer for Problem 5.

Possible answer: I rounded $879 to $900 and then added it to each answer choice; only B fit between both estimates.

Harcourt Brace School Publishers

Place Value

Write the correct answer.

1. Write the number 200 + 3 + 0.1 + 0.05 + 0.009 in standard form.

_____ **203.159** _____

2. Write the value of the digit 7 in the number 8,309.075.

_____ **0.07, or 7 hundredths** _____

3. A car dealer started the year with 600 cars on his lot. By March there were 119 cars left. How many cars had he sold?

_____ **481 cars** _____

4. At 7:00 A.M. the temperature was 22°F. By 2:00 P.M. it had risen to 41°F. By 7:00 P.M., it was 31°F. Which operation do you need to use to find the change in the number of degrees from 7:00 A.M. to 7:00 P.M.?

_____ **subtraction** _____

Choose the letter of the correct answer.

5. Which is the value of the 5 in the number 254,032,918?

A 500 million   (B) 50 million
C 5 million   D 50 thousand

6. Twenty-two vans with 10 students in each go to the basketball tournament. Three buses with 40 students in each also go to the tournament. Which is the most reasonable estimate of the number of students that attend the tournament?

A 200 students
(B) 320 students
C 2,300 students
D 120 students

7. Which shows 1,011.01 in expanded form?

F 1,000 + 100 + 1 + 0.1
G 1,000 + 100 + 1 + 0.01
H 1,000 + 10 + 0.01
(J) 1,000 + 0 + 10 + 1 + 0 + 0.01

8. When a car is warmed up, its radiator temperature is about 180°F. The boiling point of water is 212°F. How hot is the radiator before the car is warmed up?

F About 212°F
G About 180°F
H About 50°F
J About 32°F
(K) Not enough information

9. **Write About It** Explain how you found the value of the 5 in the number in Problem 5.

Possible answer: I found the place value, ten millions, and multiplied by

the value of the digit, 5, to get 50 million.

Equivalent Decimals

Write the correct answer.

1. Write *equivalent* or *not equivalent* to describe the set of decimals.

    0.05 and 0.050

    _____ **equivalent** _____

2. Write a decimal that is equivalent to 0.7.

    _____ **Possible answers: 0.70 or 0.700** _____

3. Jill estimated that there were 450 people at a concert. Lucy estimated that there were 600 people. The actual number of people was 534. Whose estimate was closer?

    _____ **Lucy's estimate** _____

4. The museum has 30 items in each display case. It has 8 display cases. Does the museum have more than 250 items or fewer than 250 item?

    _____ **fewer than 250 items** _____

Choose the letter of the correct answer.

5. Which decimal does the model show?

    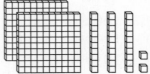

    A 1.32 **B** 0.232 **C** 0.120 **D** 0.131

6. Which is the written form of 0.707?

    F seven hundred seven thousandths
    G seventy–seven hundredths
    H seven and seven hundredths
    J seven hundred and seven thousandths

7. Which letter shows the decimal form of four hundred and four thousandths?

    A 4.04   **B** 400.040
    C 4.004   **D** 400.004

8. Fred has four coins in his pocket. The sum of the values of three of the coins equals the value of the fourth coin. Which combination of coins might Fred have?

    F 3 nickels, 1 dime
    G 2 dimes, 1 quarter, 1 nickel
    H 1 quarter, 1 penny, 1 nickel, 1 dime
    J 1 silver dollar, 2 half dollars, 1 dime
    K Not Here

9. **Write About It** Are 0.2 and 0.20 equivalent decimals? Explain.

    Possible answer: Yes; the zero to the right of the 2 does not change the

    value of the decimal.

Name _____

Comparing and Ordering

Write the correct answer.

1. Betsy wrote "forty hundredths." Katie wrote "0.4." Doug wrote "0.400." Are all three of their decimals equivalent?

_____ yes _____

2. Last year the state budget was $230 million. This year it is $221 million. Write an expression to show how you could find how much less this year's budget is.

__$230 million – $221 million__

3. Order the decimals from the least to the greatest.

77.409; 77.940; 77.49; 77.9

__77.409; 77.49; 77.9; 77.940__

4. Write >, <, or = for the ◯ to compare the decimals.

28.026 ◯ 28.206

__<__

Choose the letter of the correct answer.

5. Which group of decimals is ordered from greatest to least?
   A 34.021; 34.02; 34.002; 33.21
   B 93.22; 92.33; 94.23; 92.22
   C 0.476; 0.467; 0.046; 0.047
   D 9.54; 9.59; 9.94; 9.95

6. Which letter shows the decimal form of nine and nine hundred two thousandths?
   F 9.902   G 9.92
   H 909.002   J 9.092

7. Which number has a 1 in the hundredths place, a 2 in the tenths place, a 3 in the hundreds place, a 4 in the ones place, and a 5 in the thousandths place?
   A 123.45
   B 304.215
   C 34.215
   D 340.215
   E 340.251

8. The Cougars football team moved 95 yards down the field on three plays to win their game. On the first play they ran 28 yards. On the second play they ran 30 yards. On which play did they earn the most yards?
   F First play
   G Second play
   H Third play
   J Fourth play
   K Not Here

9. **Write About It** Explain how you found your answer to Problem 1.

__Possible answer: I drew a base-ten block model for each decimal,__

__and they were equivalent.__

Name _____

Visualizing

Sometimes it is helpful to **visualize**, or draw a mental picture, of the information in a problem. Using the details or facts to make a picture can help you organize and understand information. Read the following problem.

VOCABULARY
visualize

> Three friends compared how much apple juice they drink in one week: Sami drinks 3 cups of juice, Jane drinks 1 pint of juice, and Chris drinks 2 quarts of juice. Who drinks the most apple juice in one week?

1. Use the details to make a mental picture. Then use words to describe what you see. **Possible answers given.**

Details	**What I See**
Sami drinks 3 cups of juice.	**I pictured 3 cups.**
Jane drinks 1 pint (2 cups) of juice.	**I pictured 2 cups.**
Chris drinks 2 quarts (8 cups) of juice.	**I pictured 8 cups.**

2. Solve the problem.

   2 qt = 8 c; 1 pt = 2 c; so, 8 c > 3c > 2 c. Chris drinks the most juice.

3. Describe the strategy you used.

   Possible answer: I made a mental picture of the cups. Then I compared the amounts.

Make a mental picture of a clock or scale. Then solve the problem.

4. At the swim meet, Tiffany finished the first race in 26.490 seconds, Cora finished in 26.550 seconds, and Drew finished in 25.980 seconds. Which girl was fastest?

   Drew was fastest since the least number of sec equals fastest.

5. Mika's pumpkin weighs 7.85 lb, Grace's pumpkin weighs 7.19 lb, and Jacob's pumpkin weighs 7.92 lb. Whose pumpkin weighs the most?

   Jacob's pumpkin weighs the most.

More About Adding Decimals

Write the correct answer.

1. Write the sum.

$$3.83 + 11$$

_____ **14.83** _____

2. Write the sum.

$$4.01 + 9.327$$

_____ **13.337** _____

3. In the gymnastics finals, Cindi scores 87.949. Iris scores 87.95. Lisa scores 88.034. Kitty scores 87.909. Write the order of the gymnasts from the one with the greatest score to the one with the least score.

_____ **Lisa, Iris, Cindi, Kitty** _____

4. A basketball team scored 102 points in one game. Their star center scored 53 points. Who scored more points during the game: the center or the rest of the team combined?

_____ **The center scored more points.**

Choose the letter of the correct answer.

5. $94.029 + 7.28 = \underline{\ ?\ }$

A 101.309
B 101.057
C 101.2829
D 101.57

6. $38,000 - 7,670 = \underline{\ ?\ }$

F 31,330
G 31,430
H 30,430
J 30,330

7. Mr. Elwood has four children. The oldest is 13, and the youngest is 6. Which is the most reasonable estimate of the sum of the four children's ages?

A Between 6 and 13
B Between 13 and 20
C Between 20 and 30
D Between 30 and 45
E Between 45 and 55

8. Victor's computer is faster than Jeff's. Nora's computer is faster than Victor's. Tina's computer is slower than Nora's but faster than Victor's. What can you conclude about Tina's computer?

F It is faster than Nora's.
G It is slower than Jeff's.
H It is the slowest computer.
J It is faster than Jeff's.
K It is the fastest computer

9. Write About It Explain how you chose your answer to Problem 7.

Possible answer: I first found the least possible sum: 6 + 7 + 7 + 13 = 33;

I then found the greatest possible sum: 6 + 12 + 12 + 13 = 43.

Subtracting Decimals

Write the correct answer.

1. Write the difference.

$$6.98 - 3.28$$

_____3.7_____

2. Write the difference.

$$38.5 - 12.78$$

_____25.72_____

3. Four runners ran the 100-meter dash. Who came in third?

Charles: 12.30 seconds

Kayla: 13.25 seconds

Ed: 13.45 seconds

Bertha: 12.28 seconds

_____Kayla_____

4. Brita used a $100 bill to pay for a $79 tape player. How much change did she get back?

_____$21_____

Choose the letter of the best answer.

5. $76.69 - 40.626 = \underline{\ ?\ }$

A 36.43
B 36.036
C 37.054
(D) 36.064

6. $8.338 + 4.7 = \underline{\ ?\ }$

F 13.38
(G) 13.038
H 12.038
J 13.48

7. A plane took off and rose to 3,200 feet. It then rose another 4,500 feet. It dropped 800 feet before rising another 1,200 feet. Which expression could you use to find the plane's present altitude?

A $3,200 + 4,500 - (800 + 1,200)$
B $3,200 + 4,500 + 800 + 1,200$
C $3,200 + 4,500 - 800 - 1,200$
(D) $3,200 + 4,500 - 800 + 1,200$
E Not Here

8. A wool cap costs $3.99. Wool mittens cost $5.99. A wool scarf costs $5.59. How much would it cost to buy all three items?

(F) $15.57
G $14.57
H $13.57
J $15.97
K Not Here

9. **Write About It** Explain how you subtracted in Problem 5.

Possible answer: I first wrote 76.69 as the equivalent decimal 76.690; then

I regrouped the 9 hundredths to get 8 hundredths, 10 thousandths; then I

subtracted in each place value.

Estimating Sums and Differences

Write the correct answer.

1. Estimate the sum to the nearest tenth.

$$36.49 + 41.27$$

_____**77.8**_____

2. Estimate the difference to the nearest hundredth.

$$17.846 - 3.055$$

_____**14.79**_____

3. When Ben picks up his new car at the dealer, it has only 22.5 miles on it. By the end of the day, it has 68.8 miles on it. How many miles does Ben drive that day?

_____**46.3 mi**_____

4. The price for one gallon of gas at Station A is $1.209. At Station B, the price for one gallon is $1.199. At which station does gas cost less?

_____**at Station B**_____

Choose the letter of the correct answer.

5. Estimate each sum. Which expression has the greatest sum?

A $21.95 + 56.08$ **B** $53.71 + 28.43$
C $58.02 + 23.31$ **(D)** $55.86 + 26.94$

6. Which number is the difference of $40,000 - 23,947$?

(F) 16,053   **G** 17,153
H 16,153   **J** 63,947

7. At the grocery store, Stella buys a $2.19 bag of walnuts, a $1.89 carton of milk, and a $3.59 frozen dinner. Which is the most reasonable estimate of how much the three items will cost altogether?

A $5.00
(B) $8.00
C $10.00
D $11.00
E $12.00

8. The engineer let 3,300 gal of water out of a holding tank on Monday. She let out another 6,800 gal on Tuesday. About 1,200 gal evaporated from the tank during those two days. Which operation(s) could you use to find how much water was lost over the two days?

(F) Addition
G First addition, then subtraction
H First subtraction, then addition
J Subtraction
K Division

9. Write About It Explain how you estimated and compared to solve Problem 5.

Possible answer: I rounded to the nearest whole number, added, and

compared.

Choosing Addition or Subtraction

Write the correct answer.

1. Jeff ran the 100-meter dash in 12.94 seconds. Nguyen ran it in 13.08 seconds. How much faster was Jeff's time?

_____0.14 sec_____

2. A chemist measures 1.45 liters of solution A and 0.8 liter of solution B into a flask. How much of the mixture is in the flask?

_____2.25 L_____

3. Joan mixes 1.2 kilograms of hazelnut coffee beans with 1.55 kilograms of French roast coffee beans. Estimate the total weight of the coffee bean mixture to the nearest tenth of a kilogram.

_____2.8 kg_____

4. Matt is balancing his checkbook. He finds a mathematical mistake. His current balance is $1,485, but it should be $1,085. What amount does he have to subtract to get his actual balance?

_____$400_____

Choose the letter of the correct answer.

5. In a chorus of 64 students, there are 17 third graders and 22 fourth graders. The remaining members of the chorus are fifth graders. Which expression could you use to find out the number of *fifth graders* in the chorus?

   A $64 - (17 + 22)$
   B $64 + (22 - 17)$
   C $(22 - 17) + 64$
   D $(64 - 17) + 22$

6. Sally parks downtown at a parking meter. Parking costs $0.25 for 30 minutes. Sally expects to be parked for 3 hours. Which combination of coins will *not* be enough to cover the cost?

   F 3 quarters, 4 dimes, 4 nickels
   G 5 quarters, 1 dime, 3 nickels
   H 4 quarters, 8 dimes, 4 nickels
   J 2 quarters, 6 dimes, 8 nickels
   K Not Here

7. A gal of regular gas costs $1.29. A gal of high-test gas costs $1.43. Which expression would you use to find how much more a gallon of high-test costs?

   A $1.29 + $1.43   **B** $1.29 - $1.43
   C $1.43 + $1.29   **D** $1.43 - $1.29

8. Estimate the sum of 8.058 + 9.592 to the nearest hundredth.

   F 17   **G** 17.54
   H 17.64   **J** 17.65

9. **Write About It** Explain how you chose your answer to Problem 5.

   ___Possible answer: I needed to subtract the total number of third graders___

   ___plus fourth graders from the total number of students in the chorus.___

Synthesizing Information

When a problem presents a lot of information, it is helpful to **synthesize**, or combine, the related facts. You can group the related facts in a chart. Some charts might have more than two headings. Read the following problem.

VOCABULARY
synthesize

> Mr. Webb drove from his home to the airport. He drove 78.6 miles before lunch. He drove 201.7 miles after lunch. He drove 50.4 more miles. Then he realized he had missed the airport. He turned around and drove 11.6 miles back down the same road to the airport. How many miles was it from Mr. Webb's house to the airport?

1. Synthesize the information in the problem. Group the facts that are related in a chart. Complete the chart.

Numbers to Add	Numbers to Subtract
78.6	330.7
201.7	− 11.6
+ 50.4	

2. Solve the problem.

   <u>78.6 + 201.70 + 50.4 = 330.7; 330.7 − 11.6 = 319.1. It is 319.1 mi from Mr.</u>

   <u>Webb's house to the airport.</u>

   _____

3. Describe the strategy you used.

   <u>Possible answer: I wrote one addition sentence and one subtraction</u>

   <u>sentence.</u>

Synthesize the information. Show it in a chart. Solve. Check students' charts.

4. Kyra donated $2.85 to the Kids Care fund. Alex donated $7.55. May donated $5.00 less than Kyra and Alex combined. How much money did May donate? How much did the three students donate in all?

   <u>$5.40; $15.80</u>

5. Susanna had $58.42. She spent $6.59 for a belt and $25.83 for a pair of jeans. Then she got her allowance, which was $4.50. How much money does Susanna have now?

   <u>$30.50</u>

READING STRATEGY   PS21

Using Multiplication Properties

Write the correct answer.

1. Write the name of the multiplication property used in the number sentence.

    $$3 \times 4 = 4 \times 3$$

    _____Commutative Property_____

2. Tom jogged 2.5 miles on Monday, 3.25 miles on Wednesday, and 1.75 miles on Friday. How many miles did he jog in all?

    _____7.5 mi_____

3. Write an equivalent decimal for 6.010.

    ___Possible answer: 6.01___

4. Use a multiplication property to find the missing number.

    $$9 \times \underline{\ ?\ } = 0$$

    _____0_____

Choose the letter of the correct answer.

5. Which multiplication property is used in the number sentence?

    $$7 \times 11 = 11 \times 7$$

    (A) Commutative Property
    B Associative Property
    C Property of One
    D Zero Property

6. Which way of grouping the expression $5 \times 6 \times 7$ gives a product of 210?

    F $(5 \times 6) - 7$
    (G) $(5 \times 6) \times 7$
    H $(5 + 6) \times 7$
    J $6 \times 3 \times 7$

7. A group of shoppers enters a store together. Six of the shoppers go into the first aisle. Half of the remaining group goes into the second aisle. The other 7 shoppers go into the third aisle. How many shoppers entered the store?

    A 1 (B) 20 C 18 D 7 E 26

8. Tina builds a display of canned pumpkin pie filling. The first layer has 64 cans, the second has 32 cans, and the third has 16 cans. Tina follows this pattern until the top layer has only 1 can. How many layers are in the display?

    F 6 (G) 7 H 8
    J 9 K Not Here

9. **Write About It** Explain the method you used to solve Problem 8.

    Possible answer: Each layer has half the number of cans in the previous layer, so I kept finding half of each layer until I got to 1. Then I counted the layers.

Recording Multiplication

Write the correct answer.

1. Find the product of 3×324. Use the model to help you.

_____ 972 _____

2. Find the product of 2×513. Use the model to help you.

_____ 1,026 _____

3. A parking lot has 5 rows with 9 cars in each. The parking lot next door has 9 rows with 5 cars in each. Which parking lot has more cars?

Neither; both have the same

number of cars.

4. Pete tells Julie that he can multiply a number of any size. Julie asks him to multiply the number 123,456,789. Pete multiplies it by 0. What is the product?

_____ 0 _____

Choose the letter of the correct answer.

5. Which multiplication sentence describes the model?

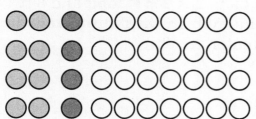

A 5×324 **B** 4×712
C 4×10 **(D)** 4×217

6. March has 31 days. If March 1 is a Friday, what day is March 31?

F Saturday   **(G)** Sunday
H Monday   **J** Tuesday
K Wednesday

7. Which multiplication sentence describes the model?

A 2×10 **(B)** 2×721
C 2×127 **D** 3×721

8. A warehouse receives 8 shipments of 180 crates each. What is the most reasonable estimate of the total number of crates received?

(F) 1,500   **G** 2,000   **H** 2,500
J 3,000   **K** 3,500

9. **Write About It** Explain how you found the answer to Problem 6.

Possible answer: A week has 7 days, so 4 weeks, or 28 days after March 1 would be a Friday. If March 29 is a Friday, March 30 is Saturday and March 31 is Sunday.

Multiplication and Area

Write the correct answer.

1. Write the product.

$$411 \times 9$$

<u>3,699</u>

2. Write the product.

$$784 \times 7$$

<u>5,488</u>

3. The hallway is 138 ft long and 9 ft wide. How many 1 ft by 1 ft tiles are needed to cover this hallway?

<u>1,242 tiles</u>

4. A *chain* is a surveyor's measure that is 792 inches long. How many inches long is a field that is 6 chains long?

<u>4,752 in.</u>

Choose the letter of the correct answer.

5. Which expression has a product of 2,496?

A 429×5 **B** 382×8

C 557×4 **(D)** 832×3

6. Which number is the product of 787×8?

(F) 6,296   **G** 6,196

H 6,026   **J** 6,926

K Not Here

7. Xenia bought a bag of cement. She used half of it to patch her front stairs. Then she used 20 pounds of it to seal a basement window. Finally, she used 15 pounds around the base of a new flag pole. She had 5 pounds left. How much cement was in the bag when Xenia bought it?

A 60 lb   **B** 5 lb

C 20 lb   **D** 120 lb

(E) 80 lb

8. The walkway to Gate 1 is 272 ft long and 6 ft wide. The walkway to Gate 2 is 204 ft long and 8 ft wide. Which walkway covers the greater area?

F Walkway to Gate 1

(G) Both have the same area

H Walkway to Gate 2

J Walkway to Gate 3

9. **Write About It** Describe the strategy you used to solve Problem 7.

<u>Possible answer: I worked backward: I started with 5 pounds, added 15,</u>

<u>and then added 20 for a sum of 40 pounds. This was half of the original</u>

<u>bag, so it was an 80-pound bag.</u>

Finding Area and Volume

Write the correct answer.

1. Write the area of a rectangle with these measurements.

$$l = 12 \text{ feet}$$
$$w = 7 \text{ feet}$$

84 sq ft

2. Write the area of a rectangle with these measurements.

5 m

24 m

120 sq m

3. An average of 63 cars per minute pass through a tunnel at rush hour. Bob stands by the entrance to the tunnel at rush hour and watches the cars go in for 5 minutes. About how many cars does he see go into the tunnel?

about 300 cars

4. A sign on an elevator says the elevator should carry no more than 1,200 pounds. Nine people get on the elevator. If each person weighs about 150 pounds, is the total weight more than the elevator should carry?

yes

Choose the letter of the correct answer.

5. Which rectangle has an area of 375 square inches.?

A l = 45 in., w = 8 in.
(B) l = 75 in., w = 5 in.
C l = 65 in., w = 6 in.
D l = 25 ft, w = 15 ft

6. What is the area of a rectangle that is 83 centimeters long and 8 centimeters wide?

(F) 664 sq cm   **G** 664 sq m
H 664 sq mm   **J** 664 cm

7. One ounce weighs a little more than 28 grams. Which of the following statements is incorrect?

A 10 oz weigh about 300 g
B 5 oz weigh about 150 g
C 7 oz weigh more than 196 g
(D) 6 oz weigh less than 168 g
E 2 oz weigh more than 56 g

8. A company's rectangular office measures 38 yards long and 9 yards wide. They have the office carpeted. The carpeting costs $5 per square yard. How much will it cost to carpet the office?

F $342   **G** $235   **H** $532
(J) $1,710   **K** Not Here

9. Write About It For Problem 6, explain what was wrong with each of the answer choices you did *not* choose.

Possible answer: They all used the wrong units or units that were not

square units.

Name _____

Analyzing Details

The details of a problem can offer clues about how to solve it. **Analyze**, or look carefully, at each part of the problem. Underline details that help you understand the problem. Read the following problem.

VOCABULARY

analyze

> Uma needs 2 square yards of fabric to make a curtain. She finds a piece of purple fabric that measures 4 ft × 5 ft. Will there be enough purple fabric to make the curtain?

1. Underline details in the problem. Then write what each detail tells you about the problem. **Possible answers given.**

Detail	**Analyze**
<u>Uma needs 2 square yards of fabric</u> to make a curtain.	"Sq yd" tells me I need to change units.
She finds a piece of <u>purple fabric that measures 4 ft × 5 ft.</u>	<u>**2 sq yd = 18 sq ft**</u> The symbol "×" reminds me <u>**I need to multiply.**</u>
<u>Will there be enough purple fabric to make the curtain?</u>	<u>**Now I can compare sq ft.**</u>

2. Solve the problem. <u>**2 sq yd = 18 sq ft; 4 ft × 5 ft = 20 sq ft; 20 sq ft is more than 18 sq ft; she will have enough purple fabric.**</u>

3. Describe the strategy you used. <u>**Possible answer: I changed yd to ft and used the formula for finding area. Then I compared the two pieces of fabric.**</u>

Underline the details. Analyze the details. Solve.

4. Jason has a <u>box measuring 2 ft × 4 ft × 3 ft.</u> He wants to pack the box with a pile of <u>clothing that has a volume of 24 cu ft.</u> Can he fit the clothes in the box? Explain.

   <u>**Yes; the volume of the box is**</u>

   <u>**24 cu ft, so the clothes will fit.**</u>

5. The <u>area</u> of Mrs. Kim's room is <u>8 ft × 10 ft.</u> She will cut a rug to fit her room. If she buys a <u>rug that measures 9 ft × 10 ft,</u> how many square feet of rug will be left over?

   <u>**10 sq ft**</u>

Multiplying by Two-Digit Numbers

Write the correct answer.

1. Find the product.

$$31 \times 28 = \underline{\ ?\ }$$

_____ 868 _____

2. Find the product.

$$44 \times 112 = \underline{\ ?\ }$$

_____ 4,928 _____

3. A tiled classroom floor measures 32 ft by 26 ft. What is the area of the classroom floor in sq ft?

_____ 832 sq ft _____

4. Andrea has a fish tank. It is 12 in. high, 20 in. long, and 10 in. deep. What is the volume of the tank in cu in.?

_____ 2,400 cu in. _____

Choose the letter of the correct answer.

5. $59 \times 78 = \underline{\ ?\ }$

(A) 4,602   **B** 4,800
C 4,502   **D** 885

6. Which multiplication problem has a product of 558?

F 47×12 **G** 25×22
(H) 31×18 **J** 44×14

7. A printer has an order to print 750 copies of a poster. She first prints 10 proof copies to check the quality. She finds a problem, so she prints 15 more proof copies. Then she prints 772 copies of the poster. How many copies of the poster does she print in all?

A 750 copies   **B** 775 copies
C 1,547 copies   **D** 47 copies
(E) Not Here

8. Mr. Vartan takes a 6:15 train every morning to work. When he gets off the train, he walks 15 minutes to his job. He gets there at 7:20 A.M. How long is his train ride?

F 45 min   **G** 35 min   **H** 55 min
(J) 50 min   **K** 65 min

9. Write About It Describe the steps you would take to multiply 46×87.

Possible answer: I would multiply by the ones, or $6 \times 87 = 522$; multiply

by the tens, or $40 \times 87 = 3,480$. Then I would add the two partial products,

regrouping if I needed to; 4,002.

Estimating Products

Write the correct answer.

1. Round each factor to its greatest place-value position. Then write an estimate of the product.

   76×428

   $80 \times 400 = 32,000$

2. Ned runs 45 km every week. How many km does he run in 52 weeks?

   _**2,340 km**_

3. Round the number 654 to its greatest place-value position.

   _700_

4. A school uniform costs $38. There are 88 students in the school. How much would it cost to buy uniforms for all of the students?

   _**$3,344**_

Choose the letter of the correct answer.

5. Which is the most reasonable estimate of the product of 97×46?

   A 5,000   **B** 500
   C 150   **D** 7,000

6. Which product is 7,200 a reasonable estimate for?

   F 8×94 **G** 67×11
   H 93×78 **J** 88×89

7. Edgar's new tape player runs on 6 "C" batteries. Each battery produces about 1.5 volts. How many volts do the batteries in Edgar's new tape player produce altogether?

   A 3 volts
   B 1.5 volts
   C 15 volts
   D 9 volts
   E 6 volts

8. Violet estimates 554×972 as about 500×900, or 450,000. Elise estimates it as about $600 \times 1,000$, or 600,000. Which statement is *not* reasonable?

   F Violet's estimate is an overestimate.
   G The product is between the two estimates.
   H Elise's estimate is an overestimate.
   J Violet's estimate is an underestimate.
   K Not Here

9. **Write About It** Explain how you chose your answer to Problem 8. **Possible answer: Violet rounded both numbers using front-end digits, so her estimate must be less than the product; Elise rounded to the greatest place-value position, so her estimate must be greater than the product.**

5th½

PS 3   #6 , #4
PS 4   #8 ✓
PS 5   #5 ✓
PS 7   #2 ✓   #7 ✓   400
PS 8   #6 ✓   400
PS 9   #6 ✓   800
PS 10   #5 ✓   400
PS 12   #1   copy
PS 13   #7 ✓
PS 14   #35 copy ~~~   2,000
PS 15   # 6 ✓
PS 17   #5 ✓ + #2
PS 18   # 5 ✓
PS 19   #2 ✓ + #6   + #8
RS 20   # 7 ✓
PS 23   #4 ✓ + (#7) copy
PS 24   #2 ✓
PS 25   # 2 ✓ + #6 ✓
PS 27   #6 ✓
PS 28   #1 ✓
PS 29   #2 ✓ + #6
PS 30   #1 + #2

$$87.76$$
$$6.28$$
$$\underline{04}$$
$$94.$$

$$\begin{array}{r} 4\,999 \\ 5\cancel{0},\cancel{000} \\ \underline{16,803} \\ 33,197 \end{array}$$

$$\begin{array}{r} 33197 \\ 16803 \\ \hline 50,000 \end{array}$$

Multiplying by Three-Digit Numbers

Write the correct answer.

1. Round each number to the greatest place-value position. Then estimate the product.

$$2,387 \times 474$$

$$\underline{2,000 \times 500 = 1,000,000}$$

2. Find the product.

$$831 \times 755 = \underline{\ ?\ }$$

$$\underline{627,405}$$

3. Karl counts 36 seats in each row. There are about 44 rows in the auditorium. About how many seats are in the auditorium?

$$\underline{\text{about 1,600 seats}}$$

4. A school will send 13 busloads of students to a field-hockey match. Each bus can hold 52 students. How many students can travel to the match on the buses?

$$\underline{\text{676 students}}$$

Choose the letter of the correct answer.

5. $287 \times 1,150 = \underline{\ ?\ }$

  A 330,050   **B** 329,950
  C 70,750   **D** 77,750

6. $432 \times 972 = \underline{\ ?\ }$

  F 419,904   **G** 1,404
  H 7,776   **J** 4,199,040

7. Jeb, Rick, and Lisa have a band. They play 3 shows in the school assembly hall. The hall can hold 350 people at a time. There are 275 people at the first show. How many empty seats are there in all for the 3 shows?

  A 350 seats   **B** 75 seats
  C 225 seats   **D** 1,050 seats
  E Not Enough Information

8. The temperature gauge in Bart's car is shown below. Which is the best estimate of the temperature it shows?

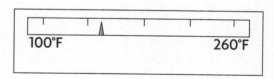

  F 100°F   **G** 110°F   **H** 140°F
  J 180°F

9. Write About It Explain how you estimated the temperature in Problem 8.

Possible answer: I subtracted 260 − 100 = 160 to find out how much the

whole dial represented; then I estimated that the needle was about $\frac{1}{4}$ of the

way, or 40°F, past 100.

Multiplying to Find Perimeter and Area

Write the correct answer.

1. Write the perimeter of the figure.

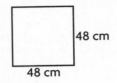

48 cm

48 cm

192 cm

2. Write the area of the figure.

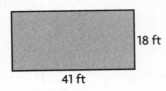

18 ft

41 ft

738 sq ft

3. Ned is a trucker. He drives about 450 miles each day. He has to make a 3,000-mile cross-country trip. Can he make it in 8 days?

yes

4. A fine china plate costs $54. Sheila orders 12 of them. How much will the plates cost altogether?

$648

Choose the letter of the correct answer.

5. What is the perimeter of the figure?

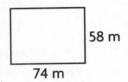

58 m

74 m

A 4,292 m   **B** 132 m
C 264 m   **D** 528 m

6. The typical worker works about 2,000 hours each year. About how many hours each year is the typical worker *not* working? (HINT: 1 day is 24 hours. 1 year is 365 days.)

A about 6,760 hr
B about 8,760 hr
C about 48,000 hr
D about 10,760 hr

7. What is the area of the figure?

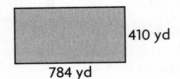

410 yd

784 yd

F 1,194 sq yd   **G** 2,388 sq yd
H 313,600 sq yd   **J** 321,440 sq yd
K Not Here

8. Leonard fences in 4 grazing fields for his livestock. Which of the fields has the greatest area for grazing?

F an 800-yd by 480-yd rectangle
G a 750-yd by 500-yd rectangle
H a 400-yd square
J a 620-yd by 370-yd rectangle

9. Write About It Explain the difference between perimeter and area.

<u>Possible answer: Perimeter measures the distance along the edge of a</u>

<u>figure; area measures the number of square units a figure covers.</u>

Paraphrasing

When you **paraphrase,** or put information into your own words, be sure to include all the important details. You can change the order of the information if it makes more sense to you. Read the following problem.

VOCABULARY
paraphrase

> The floor of Anna's dollhouse measures 24 inches by 18 inches. Her father covered the floor of the house with square tiles. Each square tile is 2 inches on each side. A box of tiles contains 125 tiles. How many tiles were left over after he covered the floor?

---

1. Write the problem in your own words. <u>Possible answer: Anna's father bought a box of 125 tiles. Each tile is 2 in. on each side, or 2 in. × 2 in. The dollhouse floor has an area of 24 in. × 18 in. How many tiles were left over from the box after he covered the floor?</u>

2. Solve the problem. <u>Find the area of the floor: 24 in. × 18 in. = 432 sq in. Each tile is 2 in. × 2 in., or 4 sq in., and 432 ÷ 4 = 108; 125 − 108 = 17; 17 tiles left.</u>

3. Describe the strategy you used. <u>Possible answer: I wrote number sentences. First, I multiplied to find the area. Then I divided the area by the area of one tile to get the number of tiles used. I subtracted that number from 125.</u>

4. Becky wants to make as big a dog run as she can. She has 92 feet of fence. What dimensions should the dog run be so that it has the greatest possible area?

   <u>23 ft x 23 ft</u>

5. A wood frame that goes around the border of a picture costs $4.35 a foot. You pay for a full foot, even if you only need part of it. Jay's picture is 15 inches by 11 inches. How much does Jay's picture frame cost?

   <u>$21.75</u>

Name _____

Placing the First Digit

Write the correct answer.

1. Estimate the quotient.

$$472 \div 8 = \underline{\ ?\ }$$

___Possible answer: 60___

2. Find the quotient.

$$757 \div 5 = \underline{\ ?\ }$$

___151 r2___

3. I am a number between 80 and 90. I am divisible by 3 and 4. What number am I?

___84___

4. A square plaza measures 85 ft on one side. What is its area?

___7,225 sq ft___

Choose the letter of the correct answer.

5. $397 \div 7 = \underline{\ ?\ }$

A 56 r5   **B** 57   **C** 565   **D** 56

6. Which is the most reasonable estimate?

$$645 \div 3 = \underline{\ ?\ }$$

F 300   **G** 21   **H** 1,800   **J** 200

7. Fernando buys a sack of animal feed. He gives one half of the feed to his cows. Then he gives 30 lb to his calves. Finally he gives the last 20 lb to the goats. What was the weight of the sack of feed he bought?

A 90 lb
B 50 lb
C 100 lb
D 200 lb
E 80 lb

8. Gwen has a table cloth with a pattern of 13 stripes of the same size on it. The table cloth is 52 in. long and 52 in. wide. Which number sentence could you use to find the area covered by one stripe?

F $52 \div (13 \div 52)$
G $52 + (52 \div 13)$
H $(52 \div 13) \times 52$
J $13 + (52 \times 52)$
K Not Here

9. Write About It Describe the method you used to solve Problem 7.

___Possible answer: I worked backward: first I added the goats' 20 lb and the___

___calves' 30 lb, then I multiplied by 2 (for the cows) to get 100 lb.___

Zeros in Division

Write the correct answer.

1. Write an estimate of the quotient.

   $671 \div 8 = \underline{?}$

   _____ **Possible answer: 80** _____

2. Find the quotient.

   $705 \div 5 = \underline{?}$

   141

3. Paul wants to put a crepe paper border around a 38 in. by 74 in. bulletin board. Write the length of crepe paper he needs.

   224 in.

4. Leona repaints an average of 16 cars each week. Write an estimate of the number of cars she repaints in 1 year. (Remember, 1 year is about 52 weeks.)

   about 1,000 cars

Choose the letter of the correct answer.

5. $473 \div 8 = \underline{?}$

   (A) 59 r1   **B** 59   **C** 465   **D** 62 r5

6. $920 \div 5 = \underline{?}$

   F 180   (G) 184   **H** 18 r4   **J** 4,600

7. $200 \div 7 = \underline{?}$

   A 28 r1   (B) 28 r4   **C** 29 r2   **D** 21

8. $810 \div 6 = \underline{?}$

   F 135 r2   **G** 132   (H) 135   **J** 137 r2

9. Clive climbed the stairs to the 23rd floor of his office building. He started on the first floor. Each flight of stairs has 13 steps. How many steps did Clive climb?

   A 299 steps   **B** 325 steps
   C 598 steps   **D** 13 steps
   (E) 286 steps

10. Harriet decides one night to count all of the stars in the sky. She falls asleep at 11:30 P.M., after counting 1,180 stars. About how many stars did she count each hour?

    F 400   **G** 800
    H 1,180   (J) Not Enough
    K 250   Information

11. **Write About It** Explain how you solved Problem 9.

    Possible answer: Clive has to climb only 22 flights of stairs to get to the

    23rd floor, so the answer is 22 × 13, or 286 steps.

Name _____

Practicing Division

Write the correct answer.

1. Use divisibility rules and write *yes* or *no* to predict whether there will be a remainder for 714 ÷ 6.

   _____ **no** _____

2. Find the quotient.

   $8)\overline{599}$

   _____ **74 r7** _____

3. A group of 6 friends earns $825 shoveling snow during the winter. If they split the money equally, how much will each one get?

   Divide; $825 ÷ 6 = $137.50 each.

4. A gallon is 128 oz. An airplane can carry 1,445 gallons of fuel. Write the number of ounces of fuel the plane can carry.

   184,960 oz

Choose the letter of the correct answer.

5. Which multiplication problem would you use to check the quotient?

   $$465 ÷ 8 = 58 \text{ r}1$$

   A $(8 + 1) \times 58$ **B** $(58 - 1) \times 8$
   C $(58 \times 8) + 1$ **D** $(1 + 8) \times 58$

6. Jake is arranging a poetry reading. There will be 6 poets. The reading should run 90 minutes. Each poet will read for the same length of time. How long will each poet read?

   F 90 min
   G 12 min
   H 20 min
   J 15 min
   K 30 min

7. Which number does not give a remainder when divided into 364?

   A 3   **B** 4   **C** 5   **D** 6

8. Claudia hunts for 4-leaf clovers. She calculates that on average she has to look at 850 3-leaf clovers for every 4-leaf clover she finds. Which number shows about how many 4-leaf clovers she could expect to find in a field of about 8,500 clovers?

   F 1
   G 10
   H 100
   J 16
   K Not Here

9. **Write About It** Explain how you could use multiplication and addition to check your answer to Problem 2.

   Possible answer: I can multiply the quotient, 74, by the divisor, 8, then add

   the remainder, 7, to the product. The sum should be equal to the dividend,

   599.

Interpreting the Remainder

Write the correct answer.

1. Use divisibility rules and write *yes* or *no* to predict whether there will be a remainder for 489 ÷ 3.

no

2. Find the quotient.

$7\overline{)595}$

85

3. A group of 275 marchers in a parade need to form rows of 8 marchers. The extra marchers lead the parade in 1 smaller row. Write the number of marchers in the first row.

3 marchers

4. Write the number of full rows of 8 marchers each there will be in the parade in Problem 3.

34 rows

Choose the letter of the correct answer.

5. How many crates are needed to ship 27 lathes if each crate can hold up to 5 lathes?

A 2   **B** 3   **C** 5   (**D**)6

6. How many full 6-oz servings can be served from an 80-oz casserole?

(**F**)13   **G** 14   **H** 2   **J** 4

7. Daryl is thinking of a two-digit number. The second digit is 8. Which of these statements about the number can you *not* be certain is true?

A The number is divisible by 2.
B The number is not divisible by 5.
C The number is greater than 17.
D The number is less than 99.
(**E**)The number is divisible by 4.

8. A florist gets an order for 250 white roses to put in 8 centerpieces. How many roses can she put in each centerpiece and how many will be left over?

F 31 roses in each, with 10 left over
G 32 roses in each, with 0 left over
H 41 roses in each, with 2 left over
(**J**) 31 roses in each, with 2 left over
K Not Here

9. **Write About It**   Write a word problem that uses division. Make the solution to your problem the remainder in the division problem.

Possible answer: Carol has 45 oranges to divide among 6 friends. If she divides them evenly, how many will she have left? 3 oranges

Interpreting Answers and Remainders

You can **interpret,** or understand the meaning of, information in the answer and in the remainder. Then you can use that information to understand what is not directly stated in the problem. Read the following problem.

VOCABULARY
interpret

> The class had 208 pencils to sell at the Fair. They bundled the pencils into equal groups. After they made the bundles, there were 5 pencils left over. How many bundles did they make? How many were in each bundle?

1. Find information about the answer and remainder. Then think about what the information suggests.

Information	The information suggests
Answer: The answer will include the number of equal groups and the number in each group.	You find the number of equal groups by dividing. I will ___divide___ to solve the problem.
Remainder: There are 5 pencils left over.	After making equal groups the remainder is ___5___. I will ___subtract___ the remainder from the total number, and then find the number of equal groups.

2. Solve the problem. 208 − 5 = 203; guess 7 bundles; 203 ÷ 7 = 29; 7 bundles with 29 pencils in each bundle or 29 bundles with 7 pencils in each bundle.

3. Describe the strategy you used to solve the problem.

   Possible answer: I guessed and checked.

Interpret the answer and remainder if any. Solve.

4. A pet store has 124 fish. There are the same number of fish in each of 7 aquariums, except for one in which there are 12 fish. How many fish are in each of the other aquariums?

   16 fish

5. Brandon has 105 baseball cards. He puts them in 9 equal groups. He has 6 cards left over. How many cards are in each equal group?

   11 cards

Name _____

Division Patterns to Estimate

Write the correct answer.

1. Write the missing number to complete the pattern.

$$350 \div 70 = 5$$
$$3{,}500 \div 70 = 50$$
$$35{,}000 \div 70 = \underline{\ ?\ }$$

_____ **500** _____

2. Frank and Joan drive 360 miles on about 8 gallons of gas. Write the average number of miles they drive per gallon.

_____ **45 miles per gallon** _____

3. Find the quotient.

$$6{,}300 \div 90 = \underline{\ ?\ }$$

_____ **70** _____

4. Ted packs 4 grapefruit in each case. He has 86 grapefruit to pack. How many will be left over?

_____ **2 grapefruit** _____

Choose the letter of the correct answer.

5. $48{,}000 \div 80 = \underline{\ ?\ }$

   A 6   **B** 60   (**C**) 600   **D** 6,000

6. $8{,}100 \div 90 = \underline{\ ?\ }$

   F 9   (**G**) 90   **H** 900   **J** 9,000

7. $6{,}300 \div 9 = \underline{\ ?\ }$

   A 7   (**B**) 700   **C** 70   **D** 7,000

8. $300{,}000 \div 6 = \underline{\ ?\ }$

   F 5,000   **G** 50   **H** 500   (**J**) 50,000

9. A truck has 8 wheels. When it is empty, it weighs 14,000 lb. When it carries a load of 42,000 lb, how much weight does each wheel carry?

   (**A**) 7,000 lb
   B 700 lb
   C 70 lb
   D 70,000 lb
   E 200 lb

10. The Markley Agency sells insurance. Their 450 clients carry an average of $4,000 worth of insurance each. The agency's goal is to add 50 clients. How many clients will they have if they reach their goal?

   F $2,000,000   **G** $1,800,000
   (**H**) 500 clients   **J** 400 clients
   K Not Here

11. **Write About It** Explain how you solved Problem 9.

   <u>Possible answer: I added 14,000 + 42,000 to find the total weight of the</u>

   <u>loaded truck; then I divided the sum by 8.</u>

Estimating Quotients

Write the correct answer.

1. Write an estimate of the quotient by using compatible numbers.

   $5{,}029 \div 68 =$ _?_

   _____ Possible answer: 70 _____

2. Write a pair of compatible numbers. Use them to estimate the quotient.

   $79\overline{)6{,}424}$

   Possible answer: $6{,}400 \div 80 = 80$

3. Koala Airlines carries an average of 272 passengers on its Dallas-Perth flight. It runs 620 such flights each year. About how many passengers does it carry on those flights each year?

   _____ About 180,000 passengers _____

4. Chester runs his horses in an octagonal pen. Each of the pen's 8 sides measures 240 ft. What is the perimeter of the pen?

   _____ 1,920 ft _____

Choose the letter of the correct answer.

5. Which expression would be best to estimate the quotient?

   $7{,}840 \div 210 =$ _?_

   Ⓐ $8{,}000 \div 200$ B $7{,}500 \div 250$
   C $9{,}000 \div 300$ D $6{,}000 \div 200$

6. Which is the most reasonable estimate of the quotient?

   $5{,}549 \div 79 =$ _?_

   F 700   G 80   Ⓗ 70   J 75

7. A group of 12 friends buys 125 concert tickets. Which of the following is not a way the tickets can be split?

   Ⓐ Each friend gets 11 tickets.
   B Each friend gets 10; 5 are returned.
   C Seven friends get 10; 5 friends get 11.
   D Five friends get 18; 7 friends get 5
   E Not Here

8. Bart can wash 53 plates in 266 seconds. About how long does it take him to wash each plate?

   F about 10 sec
   Ⓖ about 5 sec
   H about 8 sec
   J about 3 sec
   K about 2 sec

9. **Write About It**   Explain how you chose compatible numbers to estimate the quotient in Problem 2.

   Possible answer: I rounded the divisor to the nearest ten; then I looked for a

   multiple of that ten that was close to the dividend.

Placing The First Digit

Write the correct answer.

1. Write an estimate of the quotient.

$4,085 \div 38 = $ _?_

possible answer: about 100

2. Find the quotient.

$76\overline{)8,447}$

111 r11

3. Jake wants to carpet his 17-ft by 14-ft rectangular living room. How many square feet of carpeting does he need?

238 sq ft

4. A fisherman catches about 850 pounds of fish each day. About how many pounds does he catch during an 8-day run?

about 6,800 lb

Choose the letter of the correct answer.

5. Which is the most reasonable estimate of the quotient?

$38\overline{)1,894}$

A 6   **B** 5   **C** 450   **D** 50

6. $7,038 \div 94 = $ _?_

F 74 r82   **G** 74

H 156   **J** 740 r82

7. A robot moves at a speed of 1 foot each second. Which is the most reasonable estimate for the time it will take to move 1 mi? (Remember, 1 min = 60 sec, and 1 mi = 5,280 ft.)

A about 100 min
B about 1,000 min
C about 5,000 min
D about 10 min
E about 60 min

8. Eight members of a choir go to a concert by car. The others go in 6 vans each carrying 9 passengers. Which expression could you use to find the number of choir members going to the concert?

F $8 + 9 \div 6$
G $6 + 9 \times 8$
H $8 \times 6 + 9$
J $8 + (6 \times 9)$
K Not Here

9. Write About It Explain how you solved Problem 7.

Possible answer: First, I calculated that at 1 ft per second, it would take

5,280 seconds. Then, I estimated the quotient 5,280 ÷ 60 by using 6,000 ÷

60.

Correcting Quotients

Write the correct answer.

1. Write *too high*, *too low*, or *just right* for the estimate.

$$\begin{array}{r} 7 \\ 69\overline{)410} \end{array}$$

_____**too high**_____

2. Find the quotient.

$$772 \div 9$$

_____**85 r7**_____

3. Katie buys a roll of wrapping paper that is 36 in. wide. The label says the roll is 110 in. long. How many square inches are in the roll of paper?

_____**3,960 sq in.**_____

4. Felicity's pool is a 22-ft by 36-ft rectangle that is 5 ft deep. Write the number of cubic feet of water the pool will hold.

_____**3,960 cu ft**_____

Choose the letter of the correct answer.

5. $355 \div 71 = \underline{\ ?\ }$

  Ⓐ 5   **B** 4 r71   **C** 6   **D** 5 r7

6. $64\overline{)772}$

  F 12   **G** 11 r68

  H 13 r4   Ⓙ 12 r4

7. Ted rents a storage unit that has 750 cubic feet of storage space. The floor measures 8 feet by 8 feet. Which is the most reasonable estimate for the height of the storage unit?

  A 8 ft
  B 50 ft
  Ⓒ 12 ft
  D 35 ft
  E 20 ft

8. A group of 387 students travel to an art museum. One bus holds 44 students. How many buses will they need?

  Ⓕ 9 buses
  G 12 buses
  H 10 buses
  J 8 buses
  K Not Here

9. **Write About It** Describe the method you used to solve Problem 7.

_____**Possible answer: I know that the volume equals length × width × height.**_____

_____**So, 750 equals 64 sq ft × the height. I estimated (60 × 10) + (60 × 2), or**_____

_____**600 + 120; 720.**_____

Using Division

Write the correct answer.

1. Check the quotient by multiplying, and write *correct* or *incorrect*.

$$6{,}609 \div 58 = 113 \text{ r}55$$

_____**correct**_____

2. Find the quotient.

$$7{,}084 \div 73 = \underline{\ ?\ }$$

_____**97 r3**_____

3. Carol has 559 pieces of mail to deliver in 4 hours. She estimates that if she delivers 115 each hour, she will finish on time. Is her estimate reasonable?

_____**no**_____

4. Al will work 400 hours over the summer. He gets $22 for working a 4-hour shift. How much should he get for 400 hours of work?

_____**$2,200**_____

Choose the letter of the correct answer.

5. $47\overline{)3{,}887}$

A 82 r28   B 82 r33
C 72 r30   D 72 r28

6. What is the value of *n*?

$$5{,}675 \div 72 = n$$

F 78 r59   G 76 r59
H 77 r12   J 81 r12

7. Kari buys 3 goldfish at $4 each. She sees bowls marked "3 for $10" and buys 6 of them. She also buys 2 jars of fish food marked "2 for $3.00." Which expression could you use to find her total cost?

A $4 + 10 + (2 \times 3)$
B $3 \times 4 + 10 + 3$
C $3 \times 4 + (6 \times 10) + 3$
D $(3 \times 4) + (2 \times 10) + 3$
E Not Here

8. A new satellite has space available for 22 pounds of equipment. Which equipment below will fit? (HINT: 16 oz = 1 lb.)

F seven 3-lb, 3-oz items
G four 5-lb items and a 3-lb item
H twenty-four 15-oz items
J twenty 20-oz items
K a 17-lb item and ten 8-oz items

9. **Write About It** Describe the method you used to solve Problem 4.

<u>Possible answer: I used a pattern for multiplying by 10, 100, or 1,000: if</u>

<u>4 × a number is $22, then 40 × the number is $220, and 400 × the number</u>

<u>is $2,200.</u>

Choosing the Operation

Write the correct answer.

1. Write a pair of compatible numbers you could use to estimate the quotient.

$$58\overline{)9{,}329}$$

   _____possible answer: $60\overline{)9{,}000}$_____

2. Find the quotient.

$$522 \div 96 = \underline{\ ?\ }$$

   _____5 r42_____

3. Light travels about 186,000 miles per second. There are about 31,536,000 seconds in 1 year. What operation would you use to find the number of miles light travels in 1 year?

   _____multiplication_____

4. Light travels about 186,000 miles per second. The distance from the sun to Earth is about 93,000,000 miles. What operation would you use to find the number of seconds it takes light from the sun to reach Earth?

   _____division_____

Choose the letter of the correct answer.

5. Which is the most reasonable estimate of the quotient?

$$87\overline{)7{,}109}$$

   A 8 B 80 C 70 D 90

6. $728 \div 45 = \underline{\ ?\ }$

   F 17 r2   G 17 r42
   H 16 r28   J 16 r8

7. Lasers take about 1.28 seconds to reach the moon. Light travels about 186,000 miles per second. Which operation could you use to find the distance to the moon?

   A addition   B subtraction
   C multiplication D division

8. The average heart beats about 70 times per minute. If a person breathes an average of 12 times per minute, about how many times does the person breathe in 1 day?

   F 17,280 times   G 100,800 times
   H 720 times   J 6,307 times
   K Not Here

9. **Write About It** How do you know when you need to divide to solve a problem?

   Possible answer: I see that I need to find out how many equal-sized

   groups there are or how many there are in each equal-sized group.

Analyzing Details

It is helpful to **analyze,** or examine, the details in a problem. You can then use the details to help you solve the problem. Underline the details to help you remember them. Read the following problem.

> Mary Lou's parents saved money for a piano that cost $1,845. They made a down payment of $915. They paid off the remainder in 15 months, paying the same amount every month. What was their monthly payment?

1. Analyze each detail from the problem. Complete the sentence in the *Explanation* column of the table for each detail.

Detail	Explanation
The piano costs $1,845.	The total cost is $1,845.
They pay $915 down payment.	Subtract $915 from $1,845.
They pay the rest in 15 equal payments.	Divide $930 by 15.

2. Solve the problem.

   $1,845 − $915 = $930; $930 ÷ 15 = $62; Their monthly payment was $62.

3. Describe the strategy you used. **Possible answer: I wrote number**

   sentences.

Underline the details. Write a number sentence to solve.

4. It costs the press club $81.73 to print each issue of their newspaper, *School Scoop*. If they print 6 issues of the paper during the year, how much money will they spend?

   6 × $81.73 = $490.38

5. Kyla saved $108.60 in the bank in one year. She earned $7.24 in interest on the money in the bank. Kyla then took out $47.25 to buy a camera. How much did she have left in the bank?

   $108.60 + $7.24 − $47.25 = $68.59

Finding the Mean

Write the correct answer.

1. Use the stem-and-leaf plot. Write the mean for the basketball scores.

Stem	Leaves
5	2 4 4 5 8 9 9
6	0 4 5 6 7 7 7 9
7	1 1 4 5 9 9

Belle Basketball: Points Scored per Game

_____ 65 _____

2. Use the stem-and-leaf plot. Write the mean for the bike trip distances.

Stem	Leaves
3	1 2 3 6 7 8
4	0 0 2 3 9
5	2 2 2 6 7 8

Greg's 1997 Bike Trips: Miles Ridden

_____ 44 mi _____

3. Use the stem-and-leaf plot from Problem 1. Write the median for the basketball scores.

_____ 66 _____

4. Use the stem-and-leaf plot from Problem 2. Write the mode for the bike trip distances.

_____ 52 mi _____

Choose the letter of the correct answer.

5. Which is the mean for the data?

12, 28, 42, 19, 24, 12, 10

A 12   (B) 21   C 19   D 27

6. Which is the median for the data?

45, 58, 98, 37, 58, 49, 55, 27, 41

F 52   G 58   H 45   (J) 49

7. Seven friends go bowling. It costs $11 per hour for the first 2 people. Each extra person is $2 per hour. They split the cost evenly. How much will an hour of bowling cost each person?

A $2   (B) $3   C $7
D $11   E $21

8. Chuck fences in 3 rectangular fields. One is 36 yards by 42 yards. Another is 45 yards by 90 yards. The third is 38 yards by 55 yards. What is the average perimeter of the fields?

F 102 yd   G 612 yd   H 186 yd
(J) 204 yd   K Not Here

9. **Write About It**   Explain how you solved Problem 7.

Possible answer: Two people at $11 an hour means 7 − 2, or 5 extra people

at $2 per hour. 5 × $2 = $10; $11 + $10 = $21; $21 ÷ 7 = $3 per person.

Name _____

Choosing a Reasonable Scale

Write the correct answer.

1. 70, 90, 80, 100, 70, 90

You want to make a line graph to display these data. Which is the most reasonable interval to use: 1, 5, 10, or 25?

10

2. 45, 70, 65, 70, 55, 40

You want to make a line graph to display these data. Which is the most reasonable interval to use: 1, 5, 10, or 25?

5

3. Rich took 7 math tests this term. His scores were 90, 88, 75, 94, 99, 89, and 88. What was Rich's mean math test score for the term?

89

4. Look at Problem 3. Rich's teacher tells him he can choose either his mean or his median score as a final grade. Which should he choose to receive a better grade?

median (90)

Choose the letter of the correct answer.

5. Which is the median of these data?

78, 79, 57, 68, 48, 67, 58

A 65 **B** 78 **C)**67 **D** 58

6. Which is the mean of the data?

78, 79, 57, 68, 48, 67, 58

F)65 **G** 78 **H** 68 **J** 58

7. Liona finds the mean, median, and mode of her 7 math test scores. She gets 94 all three times. Which of the following is *not* a reasonable conclusion?

A She got a 94 on at least two tests.
B Half of her scores are less than or equal to 94.
C Half of her scores are greater than or equal to 94.
D The total of her scores is 658.
E) She got a 93 on all seven tests.

8. Mary, Connie, and Judy have three seats on a plane together. Mary does not want the window seat (w). Connie does not want the middle seat (m). Judy does not like the aisle seat (a). Which seating arrangement does *not* work?

F) Mary: a; Connie: m; Judy: w
G Mary: a; Connie: w; Judy: m
H Mary: m; Connie: a; Judy: w
J Mary: a; Connie: w; Judy: m
K Not Here

9. Write About It Explain how to find the mean of a set of data.

Possible answer: Count the numbers in the set; find the sum of the numbers; divide the sum by the total number of items in the set.

Making Line Graphs

Write the correct answer.

1. What would be an appropriate scale for a line graph displaying these data?

Average Monthly Temperature in Rausch

Month	Feb	Mar	Apr	May
Temp. (°F)	50	55	60	65

___0, (break), 45, 50, 55, 60, 65___

2. Plot the points from the table in Problem 1. Connect the points to show change over time.

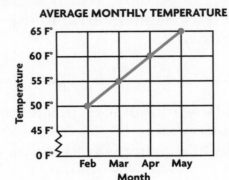

AVERAGE MONTHLY TEMPERATURE

3. Write the mean monthly temperature in Rausch for the four months shown in Problem 1.

___57.5°F___

4. Attendance at a play on 5 nights is 113, 125, 144, 98, and 155. What is the mean attendance?

___127___

Choose the letter of the correct answer.

5. Which is the mode for the data?

14, 15, 19, 15, 18, 19, 15, 14, 15

A 14   **(B)** 15   **C** 19   **D** 16

6. Which is the next number in this pattern?

18, 23, 19, 24, 20, 25, __?__

(F) 21   **G** 17   **H** 26
J 29   **K** 22

7. Which is the median for the data?

87, 91, 75, 58, 93, 98, 58, 81, 79

A 93
B 80
C 58
(D) 81

8. Tim goes shopping. He spends $30 on shoes, $12 on a tie, and $24 on a shirt. He has $6 left. How much did he start with?

F $12   **G** $60   **H** $126
(J) $72   **K** Not Here

9. Write About It Write the rule for the pattern you saw in Problem 6.

___Possible answer: As you move from each number to the next, you___

___alternate adding 5 and subtracting 4.___

Choosing the Appropriate Graph

Write the correct answer.

1. Write *line plot*, *line graph*, or *bar graph* to describe the best way to show a fifth-grader's height every month for one year.

_____ **line graph** _____

2. Write *line plot*, *line graph*, or *bar graph* to describe the best way to show the number of 1998 graduates from four high schools.

_____ **bar graph** _____

3. A group of students record their heights: 146 cm, 151 cm, 128 cm, 139 cm, and 156 cm. What is the mean of their heights?

_____ **144 cm** _____

4. What is the median of the set of data in Problem 3?

_____ **146 cm** _____

Choose the letter of the correct answer.

5. Which type of graph or plot would you choose to display the numbers of seven different kinds of flowers stored in a florist's cooler?

   A line graph
   B line plot
   C bar graph
   D circle graph

6. A 90 minute audiotape can record 45 minutes on each side. Buck records a 42 minute album on one side and a 38 minute album on the other side. How much unrecorded time does he have left on the tape?

   F 2 min   **G** 6 min
   H 10 min   **J** 8 min
   K 11 min

7. Which is the most reasonable interval to use for the scale when displaying these data on a line graph?

   15, 40, 35, 45, 25, 15, 20

   A 25   **B** 10   **C** 5   **D** 1

8. Liza is tiling a 12 foot by 18 foot room. She wants to put 1 foot square border tiles around the edge of the room. How many of these tiles will she need?

   F 30 tiles   **G** 60 tiles   **H** 58 tiles
   J 56 tiles   **K** Not Here

9. **Write About It**   Describe the strategy you used to solve Problem 8.

Possible answer: I drew a picture on grid paper and counted the number

of squares along the inside border.

Using Graphic Aids

Analyzing each part of a **graphic aid,** such as a graph, diagram, or table will help you understand the data that are presented. The title tells you about the subject. The labels on the columns and rows of a table give you more details about the subject. Read the following problem.

VOCABULARY
graphic aid

Jason surveyed students in two classes to find out which musical they wanted to perform. He organized the data in the table below. Make a graph to show which musical the students prefer.

Choices for Our Musical			
	Oklahoma!	*Funny Girl*	*Cats*
Mr. Kline's class	17	4	12
Ms. Yu's class	9	6	18

1. Answer each question about the table.
   a. What does the title tell you? **That the table will show the choices of** **musicals.**
   b. Why is there a row for Mr. Kline's class and Ms. Yu's class?
   Two classes took part in the survey. Each class's answers are in a **different row.**

2. Solve the problem. **Check students' graphs; the students prefer *Cats.***

3. Describe the strategy you used. **Possible answer: I made a double-bar** **graph to display the two sets of data in the table.**

Make a graph to display the information in the table.

4. Kyle and Patti made a table to compare the number of tickets they sold. What type of graph should they make to display the data?

   Double-bar graph; check students' **graphs.**

NUMBER OF TICKETS SOLD			
	Week 1	Week 2	Week 3
Kyle	21	42	37
Patti	33	30	29

Reading Circle Graphs

Write the correct answer. Use the circle graph for Problems 1 and 2.

1. Write the fraction of the budget spent on sets.

   $\frac{1}{4}$ **of the budget**

2. Write the total amount of money spent on programs and costumes together.

   $200

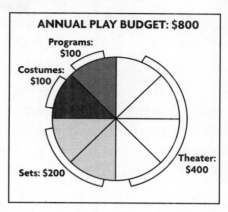

ANNUAL PLAY BUDGET: $800

Programs: $100
Costumes: $100
Sets: $200
Theater: $400

3. These are Lloyd's daily pay amounts for last week: $85, $125, $155, $100, $90. What are his mean daily earnings?

   $111

4. These are the number of students in each of the math classes this year: 15, 22, 18, 28, 7, 19, 18. Write the mode of this set of data.

   18

Choose the letter for the best answer.

5. Which type of graph or plot would be the best choice to display the population of your state over the past 40 years?

   A line graph   **B** line plot
   C bar graph   **D** circle graph

6. A band played 15 songs during a concert. Then they gave 3 encores at the end of the concert. During each encore, they played 2 songs. Which expression could you use to find the total number of songs the band played?

   A $15 \times 3 + 2$ **B** $(15 + 3) \times 2$
   C $15 + 3 + 2$ **D** $15 + (3 \times 2)$

7. Use the circle graph in Problem 1. Which letter shows the fraction of the budget spent on costumes?

   F $\frac{1}{2}$ **G** $\frac{1}{4}$ **H** $\frac{1}{3}$ **J** $\frac{1}{8}$

8. Kim has 16 dogs, 15 cats, 3 birds, 1 koala, 4 turtles, and 1 boa in her pet store. She is building display areas. She cannot have the dogs with the cats. She cannot have the cats with the birds. And she cannot have the boa with any of the other animals. What is the least number of display areas she will need?

   F 2   **G** 3   **H** 4   **J** 5

9. **Write About It**   For Problem 6, describe how answer choice B is different from choice D.

   Possible answer: The parentheses mean that the operation inside should

   be done first, so B = 18 × 2 while D = 15 + 6.

Name _____

Decimals in Circle Graphs

Write the correct answer. For Problems 1–2, use the circle graph.

1. Write a decimal to show what part of all the students are fifth graders.

   _____ 0.3 or 0.30 _____

2. Write a fraction to show what part of all the students are not sixth graders.

   _____ $\frac{6}{10}$ or $\frac{3}{5}$ _____

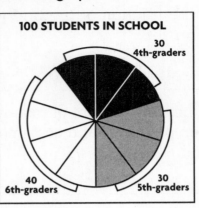

100 STUDENTS IN SCHOOL

30 4th-graders

40 6th-graders

30 5th-graders

3. Write *line plot*, *line graph*, or *bar graph* for the type of graph or plot you would use to show the number of cans of tuna sold in May in five different stores.

   _____ bar graph _____

4. Suppose you want to graph these data on a line graph: 17, 19, 8, 14, 16, 7, 19, 20. Which interval would be most reasonable for the scale: 25, 10, 5, or 1?

   _____ 1 _____

Choose the letter of the correct answer.

5. Use the circle graph in Problem 1. What part of all the students are sixth graders?

   A 0.3   B 0.4   C 0.03   D 0.04

6. Use the circle graph in Problem 1. How many students are in the entire school?

   F 200   G 70   H 100   J 1,000

7. Dan takes a two-part test. The highest score possible on each part is 800. Dan scores 710 on the first part and 730 on the second part. Which expression does *not* show how many more points he could have scored?

   A $(2 \times 800) - (710 + 730)$
   B $(800 - 710) + (800 - 730)$
   C $800 + 800 - 730 - 710$
   D $800 - 710 + 730 - 800$

8. Hannah has 7 coins in her pocket. Which amount can *not* be the value of the coins?

   F $0.27
   G $1.20
   H $0.99
   J $0.20
   K Not Here

9. **Write About It** Describe how you tested each value in Problem 8.

   __Possible answer: I started with the largest coin possible less than the given__

   __value and then tried to add smaller coins to get to the given value.__

Analyzing Graphs

Write the correct answer.

1. The data below are shown in the graph in Problem 2. Which label on the graph is incorrect?

Cougars' Highest-Scoring Games in 1998	
Date Played	**Runs Scored**
April 22	24
April 30	18
May 5	28
May 12	30

__Title should read 1998, not 1997.__

2. The graph shows the data from Problem 1. Which value has been recorded on the graph incorrectly?

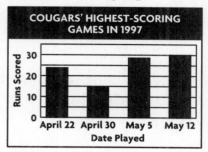

__April 30 bar should rise to 18.__

3. Use the table in Problem 1. Write the mean of the data.

_____25_____

4. Write the median of the data.

12, 15, 13, 15, 18, 27, 13

_____15_____

Choose the letter of the correct answer.

5. Suppose you want to display the data below on a line graph. Which is the most reasonable interval for the scale?

40, 50, 80, 60, 80, 100, 40

A 1   **B** 5   **C** 10   **D** 25

6. This pattern of numbers is called a *Fibonacci sequence*: 1, 1, 2, 3, 5, 8, 13, 21, 34. Every term is the sum of the two previous terms. Which is the next term in the sequence?

F 54   **G** 52   **H** 61
J 55   **K** 68

7. Which type of plot or graph would you choose to show the hourly temperature during one day?

A Line graph   **B** Line plot
C Bar graph   **D** Circle graph
E Not Here

8. Renee read 100 books. She is making a circle graph. Forty of the books were mysteries. What fraction of the circle graph should represent "Mysteries?"

F $\frac{50}{100}$ **G** $\frac{25}{100}$ **H** $\frac{80}{100}$ **J** $\frac{40}{100}$

9. Write About It Explain why you chose the type of graph you did in Problem 7.

__Possible answer: The data to be graphed show how temperature is__

__changing over time. A line graph best shows change over time.__

Comparing Graphs

Write the correct answer.

1. Write the type of graph you would use to show the number of people who come into a restaurant every day for a week.

   _____ **bar graph, or line graph** _____

2. Write the type of graph you would use to show the age of each of the last 10 presidents when he took office.

   _____ **bar graph** _____

3. How many dogs are represented by each individual section in the circle graph?

   _____ **5 dogs** _____

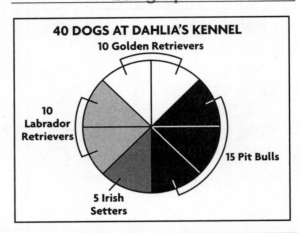

40 DOGS AT DAHLIA'S KENNEL
10 Golden Retrievers
10 Labrador Retrievers
15 Pit Bulls
5 Irish Setters

4. Use the circle graph in Problem 3. Write the fraction of the dogs that are a type of retriever.

   $\frac{1}{2}$ **of the dogs**

Choose the letter of the correct answer.

5. Which type of graph or plot would best show how your town spent its recycling budget last year?

   A bar graph   (B) circle graph
   C line graph   D line plot

6. Dahlia takes 10 spaniels at her kennel. Which of these changes will she *not* have to make to her circle graph in Problem 3?

   F Make 10 sections instead of 8.
   G Add a "10 Spaniels" label.
   (H) Move the other labels.
   J Change the title.
   K Add another color.

7. Which type of graph or plot would best show the price of soccer balls has changed in the last 10 years?

   A bar graph   B circle graph
   (C) line graph   D line plot

8. Arnie sells boxes for shipping. A large box costs $7.50, a medium box costs $5.50, and a small box costs $3.50. How much would it cost to buy 2 boxes of each size?

   F $25.00   G $30.00
   (H) $33.00   J $35.00
   K Not Here

9. **Write About It** Explain how you calculated your answer to Problem 3.

   _____ **Possible answer: I read that the total number of dogs was 40, and I saw** _____

   _____ **that this number was divided into 8 equal sections, so I divided 40 by 8.** _____

Setting a Purpose for Reading

Have you ever read a movie schedule to find out what time a movie will start? If so, you were *reading with a purpose*. Reading with a **purpose,** or goal, helps you focus on information you need. After you set a purpose, you can ask yourself questions to answer as you read. Read the instructions and problem that follow.

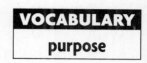

VOCABULARY
purpose

> Ms. Han's class asked 100 students where they were born. Of the students they surveyed, 0.5 were born in the community, 0.1 were born in another part of the state, 0.2 were born in a different state, and 0.2 were born in a different country. What graph would be best to display the data?

Choose the best kind of graph to display the data.

1. **a.** After reading the instructions, what purpose did you set for reading the problem? <u>**Possible answer: to think about how the information could be best shown in a graph**</u>

   b. What question did you ask yourself as you read?

   <u>**Should I make a line graph, a bar graph, a double-bar graph, or a circle graph to show the information?**</u>

2. Solve the problem. <u>**Possible answer: I chose a circle graph.**</u>

3. Describe the strategy you used. <u>**Possible answer: I made a graph; The data are given in tenths, so I knew it would be easy to show parts of a whole in a circle graph.**</u>

Set a purpose for reading. Solve.

4. The people in a neighborhood collected donations for a clothing drive. Of the items they collected, 0.3 were coats, 0.4 were shirts, 0.2 were pants, and 0.1 were hats or gloves. What graph could you use to display the data?

   <u>circle graph</u>

5. The fifth graders voted on who they wanted to represent them on the student council. The results showed that 59 students wanted Jamal, 19 students wanted Amber, and 37 students wanted Louise. What graph could you use to display the data?

   <u>bar graph</u>

Certain, Impossible, Likely

Write the correct answer.

1. Write *certain* or *impossible* to describe the chance that it will rain somewhere in the world today.

certain

2. Write *likely* or *unlikely* to describe the chance of rolling a number cube numbered 1–6 and getting a 6.

unlikely

3. The weights of the starting players on the basketball team are 114 lb, 132 lb, 95 lb, 88 lb, and 101 lb. Write the mean for the weights of the players.

106 lb

4. Edna wants to graph the number of students who visit the school library each week for a month. Would a line graph, a bar graph, or a circle graph be best for this purpose?

**Possible answers:
a bar graph or a line graph**

Choose the letter of the correct answer.

5. Which word best describes the chance of choosing a vowel if you choose a letter from the alphabet at random?

   A certain   **B** likely
   C unlikely   **D** impossible

6. Tim and Aaron are playing a board game. Each player rolls two number cubes numbered 1–6 to determine how many spaces to move. Tim has one more roll of the number cubes. He needs a total of 12 to win. Which choice best describes his chances of rolling a total of 12?

   F impossible   **G** unlikely
   H likely   **J** certain
   K Not Here

7. Which word best describes the chance of the sun rising tomorrow morning?

   A certain   **B** likely
   C unlikely   **D** impossible

8. In December, Brockton gets four snowstorms that leave 14 in., 12 in., 15 in., and 22 in. of snow. Brockton's average yearly snowfall is 56 in. How does Brockton's December snowfall compare to its yearly average?

   F It is 63 in. more.
   G It is 63 in. less.
   H It is 7 in. more.
   J It is 7 in. less.
   K It is the same.

9. **Write About It** Explain why you chose the answer you did in Problem 6.

   Possible answer: Tim needs to roll two 6's to win, and the chance of rolling any one number out of all the numbers that could come up is unlikely.

Recording Outcomes in Tree Diagrams

Write the correct answer.

1. For lunch you can order a BLT, chicken, or spaghetti. To drink, you can have orange juice, milk, or water. Write the number of choices of 1 food and 1 drink. You may make a tree diagram to help you.

_____ **9 choices** _____

2. Chuck can wear his blue shirt or his yellow shirt. He can wear his paisley tie, his silk tie, or his knit tie. Write the number of choices of shirt-and-tie combinations. You may make a tree diagram to help you.

_____ **6 choices** _____

3. Vicki earns $5 for each hour she works at her job. Write *certain*, *likely*, *unlikely*, or *impossible* to describe the chance that she will earn $2,000 at her job next week.

_____ **impossible** _____

4. Here are the number of points Michelle scored in each of her first six basketball games: 24, 12, 16, 14, 8, 16. What is the mean for the number of points she scored?

_____ **15 points** _____

Choose the letter of the correct answer.

5. A survey shows how many pets students have. Which measure would show the most common number of pets they have?

A mean   B median
(C) mode   D range

6. Sally sits down to a three-course meal. She has 3 choices for each of the courses. How many different meals are possible?

F 10 meals   (G) 27 meals
H 12 meals   J 48 meals
K 54 meals

7. Which kind of graph would be best to show the different kinds of instruments played in the school orchestra?

A line plot   B double-bar graph
C line graph   (D) circle graph

8. Which number comes next in the pattern?
93, 84, 75, 66, 57, __?__

F 49   G 38   H 66
J 46   (K) Not Here

9. **Write About It** Explain why you chose the answer you did in Problem 3.

<u>Possible answer: I divided $2,000 by the $5 per hour rate and saw that</u>

<u>Vicki would have to work 400 hours next week to earn that much,</u>

<u>which is impossible.</u>

Making Predictions

By analyzing the information in a problem, you can make
a **prediction**. A prediction is your best guess based on
information. Read the following problem.

VOCABULARY
prediction

> Ming is conducting a probability experiment. He
> tosses a penny that can land either heads up or tails
> up and spins the pointer on a spinner divided into 6
> equal sections, labeled 1–6. How many possible
> outcomes are there for this experiment? What are the
> possible outcomes?

Answer the following questions to help you make predictions.

1. List the information in the problem that will affect the
   outcomes. __The penny has heads and tails; the spinner has__
   __six sections, labeled 1-6.__

2. How many possible outcomes can there be when Ming
   tosses the penny? How many possible outcomes can there
   be when he spins the pointer? __Two possible outcomes of tossing the__
   __penny; six possible outcomes of spinning the pointer__

3. Solve the problem. __There are 12 possible outcomes: 1H, 2H, 3H, 4H, 5H,__
   __6H, 1T, 2T, 3T, 4T, 5T, 6T.__

4. Describe the problem-solving strategy you used. __Possible answer:__
   __I made a tree diagram to show the possible outcomes.__

Underline the infomation that will help you predict outcomes.
Solve each problem.

5. Emile can choose to take *either chorus or band* in the
   morning. He can take *track, gymnastics, or wrestling* in the
   afternoon. What are the combinations Emile can take? __chorus and track,__
   __chorus and gymnastics, chorus and wrestling, band and track, band and__
   __gymnastics, band and wrestling__

6. Jean plans costumes for *5 actors*. She has *5 hats: 1 blue,
   1 red, 1 white, 1 black, and 1 green*. Each actor will wear
   either a *brown or grey shirt*. How many possible color
   combinations could the actors wear? __10 possible combinations__

Name _____

Finding Probability

Write the correct answer.

1. Write a fraction for the probability of pulling a black marble if you pull a marble from the bag without looking.

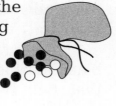

$$\frac{7}{10}$$

2. Write the probability of spinning white if you spin the pointer once.

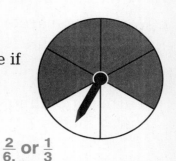

$$\frac{2}{6}, \text{ or } \frac{1}{3}$$

3. Write *certain*, *likely*, *unlikely*, or *impossible* to describe the chance of picking an orange marble from the bag in Problem 1.

impossible

4. Write *certain*, *likely*, *unlikely*, or *impossible* to describe the chance of spinning either grey or white if you spin the pointer in Problem 2.

certain

Choose the letter of the correct answer.

5. There are 12 names in a hat. Keesha's name is one of them. A name is picked without looking. What is the probability that Keesha's name will be picked?

A $\frac{1}{2}$ **B** $\frac{12}{12}$ **Ⓒ** $\frac{1}{12}$

D $\frac{3}{5}$ **E** Not Here

6. Toni had to climb the stairs to her 11th floor office. Each flight of stairs has 19 steps with an extra 2 steps on each landing. How many steps did she climb?

F 198   **G** 231

H 200   **Ⓙ** 210

7. Jim has to take a physical science course, a life science course, and a social science course. How many different combinations of courses can he take?

Physical Science	physics, chemistry, astronomy, geology
Life Science	biology, anatomy, physiology
Social Science	sociology, political science, psychology

A 12   **B** 24   **C** 27

D 32   **Ⓔ** 36

8. Write About It Explain how you solved Problem 6.

Possible answers: I drew a picture to find out how many stairs Toni

climbed; I added 19 + 2 = 21 and then multiplied by 10 floors, or 210 steps.

Comparing Probabilities

Write the correct answer.

1. You pull a marble without looking. Which outcome is more likely, pulling a black marble or pulling a gray marble?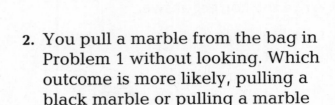

   _____ picking a black marble _____

2. You pull a marble from the bag in Problem 1 without looking. Which outcome is more likely, pulling a black marble or pulling a marble that is not black?

   picking a marble that is not black

3. You pull a marble from the bag in Problem 1 without looking. Write a fraction for the probability of pulling a white marble.

   $$\frac{4}{13}$$

4. Zane gets these scores on his science exams one term: 93, 100, 88, 94, 100. Write his mean grade for the exam scores.

   95

Choose the letter of the correct answer.

5. You pull a marble from the bag in Problem 1 without looking. Which word best describes your chance of pulling a red marble?

   (A) impossible   B unlikely
   C likely   D certain

6. Which would be the best type of graph to show the change in height of a student from fourth grade to eighth grade?

   F line plot   (G) line graph
   H bar graph   J circle graph

7. You pull two marbles from the bag in Problem 1 without looking. How many possible outcomes are there?

   A 9   (B) 6   C 4
   D 27   E 36

8. Which number comes next in the pattern?

   87, 92, 102, 117, 137, _?_

   F 147   G 152   H 157
   (J) 162   K Not Here

9. **Write About It** Write a rule for the pattern you found in Problem 8.

   Possible answer: As you move along to the next number, you add 5 to the

   previous number, then 10, then 15, and so on.

Name _____

LESSON
12.2

Patterns in Decimal Factors and Products

Write the correct answer.

1. Write the missing number. Use the pattern to help you.

$1 \times 9 = 9$
$0.1 \times 9 = 0.9$
$0.01 \times 9 = \underline{?}$

_____ **0.09**

2. Write the missing number. Use the pattern to help you.

$240 \times 1 = 240$
$240 \times 0.1 = \underline{?}$
$240 \times 0.01 = 2.40$

_____ **24.0**

3. Gum is $0.45 per pack. Is $2.00 enough to buy 4 packs?

_____ **yes**

4. Bill glues 8 plastic strips on top of each other. The strips are each 0.9 centimeters thick. How thick is the final strip?

_____ **7.2 cm**

Choose the letter of the correct answer.

5. Malcolm empties his change jar. He counts 380 pennies and 110 dimes. Which expression can he use to find the total value of the change?

A $(380 \times 110) + (\$0.1 \times \$0.01)$
B $(\$0.1 + \$0.01) \times (380 + 110)$
C $(\$0.01 \times 380) + (\$0.010 \times 110)$
D $(\$0.1 \times 380) + (\$0.01 \times 110)$
E $(\$0.01 \times 380) + (\$0.10 \times 110)$

6. A dance troupe wants to have 96 dancers on stage during a performance. Which of the following arrangements will *not* use all of the dancers?

F 8 rows of 12
G 3 rows of 16 and 6 rows of 8
H 7 rows of 12 and 2 rows of 6
J 5 rows of 16 and 1 row of 12
K Not Here

7. Which number completes the pattern?

$1 \times 36 = 36$
$0.1 \times 36 = 3.6$
$0.01 \times 36 = \underline{?}$

A 0.36 B 0.036 C 360 D 0.306

8. Which product is greatest?

F 6×0.5
H 0.05×6
G 6×0.05
J 6×5.0

9. **Write About It** Describe a pattern you can use to solve Problem 7.

Possible answer: Each time the decimal point in the first factor moves one place to the left, the decimal point in the product moves one place to the left.

Harcourt Brace School Publishers

Multiplying a Decimal by a Decimal

Write the correct answer.

1. Write the number that will complete the multiplication sentence for the decimal model.

$0.3 \times 0.6 = $ __?__

_____ **0.18** _____

2. Write the number that will complete the multiplication sentence for the decimal model.

$0.5 \times $ __?__ $= 0.40$

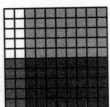

_____ **0.8** _____

3. Nestor notices that 41 dollar bills can be written as $41.00 and that 41 dimes can be written as $4.10. Use the pattern to show how 41 pennies can be written.

_____ **$0.41** _____

4. Jayne has 2 rolls of 50 dimes each. She has another 36 dimes left. How much money in dimes does Jayne have altogether?

_____ **$13.60** _____

Choose the letter of the correct answer.

5. Which number is the product of 0.7×0.9?

A 63   **B** 6.3   **C** 0.63   **D** 0.063

6. Which number is the product of 0.2×0.5?

F 0.0010   **G** 0.010   **H** 0.10   **J** 1.0

7. Zelda is taking a trip to two countries. She can spend the first week in Denmark, Norway, or Sweden. She can spend the second week in Switzerland, France, Spain, or Italy. How many choices does she have ?

A 3   **B** 9   **C** 12   **D** 18

8. A farmer plants 0.5 of a field with corn. Of that corn, 0.6 is sweet corn. What part of the field is planted in sweet corn?

F 0.5   **G** 0.6   **H** 0.30
J 0.03   **K** Not Here

9. Write About It Explain what each gray area in the model in Problem 1 represents.

Possible answer: Each of the lighter gray areas represent the factors, 0.3

and 0.6. The darkest gray is the product, or 0.18.

Harcourt Brace School Publishers

Sequencing

Noticing the order, or **sequence,** in which things happen can help you understand a problem. As you read, think about what happens first, next, and last. Then think about how this sequence helps you solve the problem. Read the following problem.

> Dea painted the background of her poster dark blue. Then she painted stars on 0.8 of the poster. Finally, she put glitter on 0.3 of the stars. What part of the poster had glitter on the stars?

1. Dea wrote down the steps to solve the problem in the order in which they occurred. Write how the sequence gives you clues about how to solve the problem.

STEPS TO SOLVE THE PROBLEM	WHAT THE STEPS TELL ME
Step 1: Dea paints stars on 0.8 of the poster	Possible response: First, Dea paints $\frac{8}{10}$ of the poster with stars.
Step 2: Dea puts glitter on 0.3 of the stars.	Possible response: Next, Dea puts glitter on $\frac{3}{10}$ of the part of the poster that has stars on it.
Step 3: What part of the poster had glitter on the stars?	Possible response: I need to find part of a part. I can multiply.

2. Solve the problem. <u>$0.8 \times 0.3 = 0.24$; 0.24, or $\frac{6}{25}$, of the</u>

<u>poster has glitter on the stars.</u>

3. Describe the problem-solving strategy you used. <u>Possible</u>
<u>answer: I made a model showing the sequence of steps</u>
<u>in the problem so I could see the overlap of the parts.</u>

Use sequence to help you solve these problems.

4. Ana cut a pizza into 8 equal pieces. She put mushrooms on 0.5 of the slices. Then she put ham on 0.4 of the slices that had mushrooms on them. What part of the pizza had mushrooms and ham?

<u>0.2 of the pizza</u>

5. Matt planted his garden. He planted lettuce in 0.3 of the garden. Then he planted radishes in 0.2 of the part of the garden that he planted with lettuce. What part of the garden had lettuce. and radishes planted in it?

<u>0.06 of the garden</u>

Placing the Decimal Point

Write the correct answer.

1. Use estimation to place the decimal point in the product.

$$34 \times 0.7 = 238$$

_____**23.8**_____

2. Use estimation to place the decimal point in the product.

$$34 \times 0.07 = 238$$

_____**2.38**_____

3. In Carol's basement, 0.8 of the area is a family room and 0.4 of the family room is a game area. How much of the basement is a game area?

_____**0.32 of the basement**_____

4. Ron is a salesperson. He gets 0.01 of each sale in commission. When he sells a $750 item, how much commission does he receive?

_____**$7.50**_____

Choose the letter of the correct answer.

5. Which is the best estimate for the product of 46×0.6?

Ⓐ 23   **B** 2   **C** 12   **D** 276

6. Sound travels about 1 mile in 5 seconds. Gerry is watching fireworks. After a flash, the sound takes about 15 seconds to reach her. About how far away are the fireworks?

A About 1 mi   **B** About 2 mi
Ⓒ About 3 mi   **D** About 4 mi

7. Which is the best estimate for the product of $\$0.45 \times 8$?

F $36   **G** $45   Ⓗ $4   **J** $1.25
K $40

8. Which situation best describes what this graph shows?

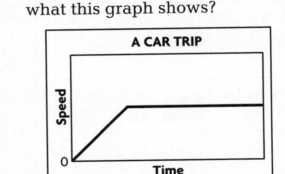

A CAR TRIP

F The car speeds up, then slows down.
Ⓖ The car speeds up, then drives at a steady speed.
H The car drives away, then stops.
J The car drives up a hill, then on a level road.
K Not Here

9. **Write About It** Explain how you solved Problem 4.

Possible answer: I used a pattern: 750 × 1 = 750;

750 × 0.1 = 75.0; 750 × 0.01 = 7.50.

More About Placing the Decimal Point

Write the correct answer.

1. Estimate the product.
   $$72 \times 0.4$$

   _____ Possible answer: 35 _____

2. Estimate the product.
   $$0.68 \times 64$$

   _____ Possible answer: 40 _____

3. Lara has 7 rolls of dimes. Each roll has 50 dimes. What is the total value of Lara's dimes?

   _____ $35.00 _____

4. Hannah is stacking boxes. Each box weighs 6.5 kg. Should she stack 5 boxes on a shelf designed to hold no more than 30 kg?

   _____ no _____

Choose the letter of the correct answer.

5. $0.38 \times 24 = \underline{\ ?\ }$
   - (A) 9.12
   - B 0.912
   - C 91.2
   - D 912

6. Which number completes the pattern?

   44, 55, $\underline{\ ?\ }$, 110, 154, 209
   - F 66
   - (G) 77
   - H 88
   - J 99
   - K 110

7. $2.06 \times 19 = \underline{\ ?\ }$
   - A 0.3914
   - B 3.914
   - (C) 39.14
   - D 391.4

8. Sheila plays a word-guessing game. She needs to spend points to buy each letter she guesses. So far she has guessed these letters: G, P, E, D, A, R. A vowel costs twice as much as a consonant. She has spent 400 points. How many points does each vowel cost?
   - F 200 points
   - G 25 points
   - H 50 points
   - (J) 100 points
   - K Not Here

9. **Write About It** Explain your strategy for solving Problem 4.

   Possible answer: First I rounded 6.5 to 7; 7 × 5 = 35,

   which is too much. So I rounded 6.5 to 6: 6 × 5 = 30.

   I knew the total weight had to be more than 30 kg,

   so it was too much.

Multiplying Mixed Decimals

Write the correct answer.

1. Write the product.

   $3.56 \times 2.8 =$ __?__

   _____ 9.968 _____

2. Write the product.

   $\$22.84 \times 5.5 =$ __?__

   _____ $125.62 _____

3. Sales tax is $0.04 on each dollar. How much will it cost Neville to buy a $6.75 hat?

   _____ $7.02 _____

4. If the average family has 2.3 children, how many children would you expect in 100 families?

   _____ 230 children _____

Choose the letter of the correct answer.

5. Hans's trip to work is 6.8 km. He makes the trip twice a day, 6 days a week. Which distance shows how far he commutes in 1 week?

   A 816 km
   B 68 km
   C 680 km
   (D) 81.6 km

6. What is the cost of 12 turtlenecks at $14.90 each, with $0.05 tax on each dollar?

   F $1,877.40   G $1,788.00
   H $89.40   (J) $187.74

7. Brad fills up his car's tank with 8.5 gallons of gasoline at $1.48 per gallon. How much change should he get from a $20 bill?

   A $6.32
   B $12.58
   C $8.42
   (D) $7.42
   E Not Here

8. When Eleanor gets her paycheck, she deposits half of it into the bank. She then spends $78.76 on groceries and $560 on rent. She has $48.50 left. What was the amount of her paycheck?

   (F) $1,374.52
   G $1,249.34
   H $116.92
   J $2,048.84
   K Not Here

9. **Write About It** Describe the strategy you used to solve Problem 8.

   Possible answer: I worked backward: I added $48.50

   to the $560 rent and the $78.76 for groceries, and

   then I multiplied the sum by 2.

Patterns in Decimal Division

Write the correct answer.

1. Linda's new printer can print 600 pages per hour. Her old printer could print 240 pages per hour. How many pages per minute faster is her new printer than her old printer?

   6 pages per minute

2. A room has 2 rugs. One rug covers 0.8 of the room. A second rug covers 0.5 of the amount covered by the first rug. How much of the room is covered by the second rug?

   0.40

3. Write the quotient.

   $60 \div 8 =$ _?_

   7.5

4. Bob earns $158.50 for 1 day of work. How much does he earn for 0.5 day of work?

   $79.25

Choose the letter of the correct answer.

5. What is the missing quotient for these number sentences?

   $900 \div 400 =$ _?_
   $90 \div 40 =$ _?_
   $9 \div 4 =$ _?_

   A 2,250 **B** 225 **C** 22.5 (**D**)2.25

6. Verne has a wheel of cheese 20 in. in diameter. He cuts it into 8 equal wedges. He wants to put them into a square box, so that the points of 2 wedges fit into each corner of the box. Which is the smallest box all 8 pieces would fit in?

   A a square box with 10 in. sides
   (**B**) a square box with 20 in. sides
   C a square box with 40 in. sides
   D a square box with 8 in. sides
   E a square box with 16 in. sides

7. What is the missing quotient for these number sentences?

   $1,000 \div 800 =$ _?_
   $100 \div 80 =$ _?_
   $10 \div 8 =$ _?_

   F 0.0125   **G** 0.125
   H 12.5   (**J**)1.25

8. Arturo sees this pattern on his calculator: $1,000 \div 8 = 125$
   $100 \div 8 = 12.5$
   $10 \div 8 = 1.25$.

   What quotient will he get when he enters $1 \div 8$?

   (**F**) 0.125   **G** 0.0125   **H** 0
   J 0.00125   **K** Not Here

9. **Write About It** Describe the pattern in the quotients in Problem 8.

   Possible answer: As the decimal point in the dividend moves one place to the left, the decimal point in the quotient also moves one place to the left.

Classifying and Categorizing

When you read a problem, it is helpful to see if you can **classify** the information in the problem into a category. The things in a **category** have something in common, such as the operations addition, subtraction, multiplication or division. As you read, look for words and phrases that are clues to which operation you can use.

VOCABULARY

classify
category

CATEGORIES			
ADDITION	**SUBTRACTION**	**MULTIPLICATION**	**DIVISION**
In All	More Than	In All Groups	In 1 Group

What words help you categorize this problem?

> Daisy is the class treasurer. She needs to give <u>equal amounts</u> of money to four class committees. There is $125.00 in the class treasury. How much money will each committee receive?

1. Write some other words that give clues about each category of problems.   **Possible answers given.**

   Addition Problems   <u>**altogether, and, total**</u>

   Subtraction Problems   <u>**less than, fewer than, difference, compare, take away**</u>

   Multiplication Problems   <u>**total of groups**</u>

   Division Problems   <u>**equal groups, in each group**</u>

2. Solve the problem. In which category—addition, subtraction, multiplication, or division—does this problem fit?   <u>**$125 ÷ 4 =**</u>

   <u>**$31.25. Each committee will receive $31.25; division.**</u>

3. Describe the problem-solving strategy you used.   <u>**I wrote a number**</u>

   <u>**sentence.**</u>

Name the category. Solve.

4. Mike went to the grocery store to buy fruit. He bought 3 mangos for $2.76 and a sack of oranges for $4.89. How much money did he spend in all?

   <u>**Addition problem;**</u>

   <u>**he spent $7.65.**</u>

5. Amber's mother gives her $4.75 each week for an allowance. Amber plans to save all of her allowance for 6 weeks. How much money will she have saved?

   <u>**Multiplication problem;**</u>

   <u>**she will have saved $28.50.**</u>

Harcourt Brace School Publishers

Dividing Decimals by Whole Numbers

Write the correct answer.

1. Write the quotient.

   7.2 ÷ 9 = __?__

   _____ 0.8

2. Write the quotient.

   3.43 ÷ 7 = __?__

   _____ 0.49

3. Three servers in a restaurant split their tips equally. One Saturday night they make $390 total. The next Tuesday, they make a total of only $39. How much more did each server make in tips on Saturday than on Tuesday?

   _____ $117.00

4. Rhonda calls her brother in New York. She pays $0.25 per minute. If she stays on the phone for 14 minutes, how much is she charged?

   _____ $3.50

Choose the letter of the correct answer.

5. A dancer starts at the back of a 22-ft wide stage. She moves toward the front of the stage by repeating this pattern: she steps 4 feet forward, then 2 feet back. She continues until she gets to the front of the stage. How many times does she have to repeat the pattern?

   A 10 times **B** 5 times
   C 11 times **D** 8 times
   E 22 times

6. A train heads west at 90 miles per hour. A train on an adjacent track heads east toward the first train at 80 miles per hour. At 1:00 P.M., the trains are 85 miles apart. If they both keep a constant speed, how far apart will they be at 1:30 P.M.?

   F 0 mi **G** 42.5 mi
   H 85 mi **J** 170 mi
   K Not Here

7. What is the quotient?

   7)4.97

   A 0.71 **B** 7.1 **C** 0.071 **D** 71

8. What is the quotient?

   38.45 ÷ 5 = __?__

   F 7.69 **G** 7.56 **H** 7.89 **J** 7.9

9. **Write About It** Explain your solution to Problem 5.

   Possible answer: I drew a picture on grid paper. After 10 repetitions

   she will be at the front of the stage.

Placing the Decimal Point

Write the correct answer.

1. Use estimation to place the decimal point in the quotient.

$$\begin{array}{r} 0\ 32 \\ 8\overline{)2.56} \end{array}$$

_____ **0.32** _____

2. Use estimation to place the decimal point in the quotient.

$$\begin{array}{r} 6\ 41 \\ 6\overline{)38.46} \end{array}$$

_____ **6.41** _____

3. Pam spent $44.58 each for uniforms for the field hockey team. She bought 8 uniforms. How much did she spend?

_____ **$356.64** _____

4. Chandra has 16.4 kg of plant fertilizer. She wants to divide it evenly among 4 flower beds. How much should she put on each flower bed?

_____ **4.1 kg** _____

Choose the letter of the correct answer.

5. What is the quotient?
$$9\overline{)8.28}$$
Ⓐ 0.92   **B** 9.2   **C** 0.092   **D** 92

6. What is the quotient?
$$38.7 \div 6 = \underline{\ ?\ }$$
F 6.25   **G** 6.35   **H** 6.4   Ⓙ 6.45

7. Florence buys 4 shirts. Her total cost, with tax, is $93.87. The tax is $4.47. What is the cost of each shirt before tax?

A $89.40   **B** $4.47   Ⓒ $22.35
D $23.47   **E** $93.87

8. A train heads west at 90 miles per hour. Another train on the same track is in front of the first train. It heads west at 60 miles per hour. At 2:00 P.M., the trains are 75 miles apart. If they both keep a constant speed, how far apart will they be at 2:30 P.M.?

F 0 mi   Ⓖ 60 mi   **H** 75 mi
J 150 mi   **K** Not Here

9. **Write About It** Explain how you solved Problem 8.

Possible answer: I drew a diagram, so I could see that the faster train

would be catching up to the slower train. After half an hour, the faster

train would have gone 45 miles and the slower, 30 miles; so they would

be 15 miles closer together.

Choosing the Operation

Write the correct answer.

1. For exercise, Lila walks 3.5 km each day. How far does she walk in 5 days?

_____ **17.5 km**

2. Ron biked 45.55 km last week. He biked the same distance each day for 5 days. How far did he bike each day?

_____ **9.11 km**

3. Write the quotient.
$3.78 \div 7 =$ ___?___

_____ **0.54**

4. Write the quotient.
$9\overline{)29.7}$

_____ **3.3**

Choose the letter of the correct answer.

5. Katy buys 5 pounds of chicken to split evenly with two of her sisters. They want to know how much chicken each of them should get. Which operation could you use to solve this problem?

A addition   **B** subtraction
C multiplication   **(D)** division

6. Katy is making a recipe that calls for $\frac{3}{4}$ lb of chicken. The recipe serves 4 people. Katy wants to make the recipe for 12 people. Which operation could you use to calculate the amount of chicken Katy needs to use?

F addition   **G** subtraction
(H) multiplication   **J** division

7. Chip takes the 11:56 A.M. bus from Kankakee to Peoria. How long can he expect to be on the bus?

BUSES FROM KANKAKEE TO PEORIA			
Depart Kankakee	9:56 A.M.	11:56 A.M.	12:56 P.M.
Arrive Peoria	12:41 P.M.	2:48 P.M.	4:03 P.M.

A 3 hr, 15 min   **(B)** 2 hr, 52 min
C 3 hr, 52 min   **D** 3 hr, 8 min

8. A truck travels west at 60 miles per hour. Another truck is ahead of the first truck on the same road. It heads west at 40 miles per hour. At 3:00 P.M., the trucks are 40 miles apart. If they both keep a constant speed, at what time will the first truck catch up with the second?

F 3:00 P.M.   **G** 3:30 P.M.
(H) 5:00 P.M.   **J** 4:30 P.M.
K Not Here

9. Write About It Explain how you chose your answer to Problem 7.

Possible answer: I started with 11:56 A.M., added on 4 minutes to get to

noon, then added on 2 hr 48 min to get to 2:48 P.M. for a total of 2 hr 52 min.

Linear Units

Write the correct answer.

1. Choose the most reasonable unit for measuring the width of a dollar bill. Write *mm*, *cm*, *dm*, *m*, or *km*.

_____ **cm** _____

2. Choose the most reasonable unit for measuring the distance across your state. Write *mm*, *cm*, *dm*, *m*, or *km*.

_____ **km** _____

3. A 5-axle truck pays a toll of $14.35. The toll is charged by the axle. How much would a 2-axle car pay?

_____ **$5.74** _____

4. If 1 ream of paper is 1.85 inches thick, how tall does the box need to be to hold a stack of 6 reams?

_____ **11.1 in.** _____

Choose the letter of the correct answer.

5. Which is the most reasonable unit for measuring the thickness of a floppy disk?

Ⓐ mm   **B** cm   **C** m   **D** km

6. Which is the most reasonable unit for measuring the length of a swimming pool.

F mm   **G** cm   Ⓗ m   **J** km

7. Ericka plays a piece of piano music at a tempo of about 72 beats per minute. The piece takes her 3 minutes to play. Which tempo would make the piece take 4 minutes to play?

A 96 beats per minute
B 108 beats per minute
C 48 beats per minute
Ⓓ 54 beats per minute
E 36 beats per minute

8. A biker finishes a race in 22 min, 20 sec, but has 100 sec added to his time for missing a turn. Which expression could you use to find the biker's time—in minutes—after the penalty is applied?

F $(22 \times 60 + 20 - 100) \div 60$
Ⓖ $(22 \times 60 + 20 + 100) \div 60$
H $(22 \times 60 + 20 + 100) \times 60$
J $(22 \times 60 + 20 - 100) \times 60$
K Not Here

9. **Write About It** Explain the method you used to solve Problem 7.

Possible answer: If a 72 beats per minute tempo lasts for

3 minutes, it lasts for 216 beats. To make 216 beats last

for 4 minutes, play it at 216 ÷ 4, or 54, beats per minute.

Units of Mass

Write the correct answer.

1. Choose the measure of the object's mass that is more reasonable.
   110 g or 110 kg

   _____ **110 kg** _____

2. Choose the measure of the object's mass that is more reasonable.
   500 mg or 500 g

   _____ **500 mg** _____

3. Charles is the state javelin champ. Which is the most reasonable unit to use to measure the length of his best javelin throw: mm, cm, m, or km?

   _____ **m** _____

4. Nikita is repairing a wrist watch. She finds that a spring is broken. Which unit of measure, mm, m, or km, is the most reasonable for the length of the spring?

   _____ **mm** _____

Choose the letter of the correct answer.

5. Which is the most reasonable unit to use to measure the mass of a pickup truck?

   A mg   **B** g   **C** kg   **D** km

6. Which is the most reasonable unit to use to measure the mass of a flute?

   F mg   **G** g   **H** kg   **J** cm

7. An old cheer starts, "Two bits, four bits, six bits, a dollar." If a dollar is worth 8 bits, what is the value of 1 bit?

   A $0.25   **B** $0.10   **C** $0.0625
   D $0.125   **E** $8.00

8. Wesley needs to move 820 kg of grain across the river in a canoe that can carry no more than 120 kg. Wesley himself has a mass of 70 kg. What is the least number of river crossings he will have to make?

   F 17 crossings   **G** 18 crossings
   H 32 crossings   **J** 33 crossings

9. **Write About It** Explain how you got your answer to Problem 8.

   Possible answer: I subtracted 70 kg from 120 kg to get 50 kg, the amount of

   grain the canoe could carry on each crossing. Then I divided 820 by 50 to get

   16 round trips, or 32 crossings, with a remainder of 20 kg for 1 final crossing.

Name _____

Relating Metric Units

Write the correct answer.

1. Write the equivalent measurement.

5 kilograms = __?__ grams

_____5,000_____

2. Write the equivalent measurement.

9 centimeters = __?__ meters

_____0.09_____

3. Anna is taking her liquid cold medicine. Which is the most reasonable unit for her to use when measuring one dose: mL, L, or kL?

_____mL_____

4. Phil is weighing flour to use to bake a cake. Which is the most reasonable unit for him to use: mg, g, or kg?

_____g_____

Choose the letter of the correct answer.

5. Which is the most reasonable measurement?

A 180 g   B 180 mg
C 180 kg   D 180 km

6. Which group of measurements is ordered from shortest to longest?

F 9 mm, 9 km, 9 cm, 9 m
G 9 cm, 9 km, 9 m, 9 mm
H 9 km, 9 m, 9 cm, 9 mm
J 9 mm, 9 cm, 9 m, 9 km

7. Rhea and Luis go fishing. Rhea catches a trout that she measures as 26 cm long. Luis catches a bass that he measures as 260 mm long. Which of the following is true?

A Rhea caught the longer fish.
B Luis caught the longer fish.
C Both fish are the same length.
D Both should use km to measure.
E Both should use m to measure.

8. Lee wants to be a weight lifter. He has been training for the past year for his first meet. He weighs himself and sees that he is much heavier than he was last year. Which is the most reasonable measure of the amount of weight Lee might have gained?

F 2,500 mg
G 250 g
H 250 kg
J 25 kg

9. Write About It Explain why you made the choice you did in Problem 8.

Possible answer: 2,500 mg is only the mass of a few paper

clips; 250 g is about the mass of an orange; 250 kg is the

mass of several people together; 25 kg is reasonable.

Changing Units

Write the correct answer.

1. Write the missing unit.

6,870 g = 6.87 __?__

_____ kg

2. Write the equivalent measurement.

6.2 m = __?__ cm

_____ 620

3. Doug buys 4 boxes of cereal for a total of $12.76. If each box cost the same amount, what was the cost of 1 box of cereal?

_____ $3.19

4. Gwendolyn hooks together 6 pieces of model railroad track. Each track is 22.5 cm long. How long is the combined length of the track?

_____ 135 cm

Choose the letter of the correct answer.

5. If room on a space shuttle flight rents for $1 for 1 cu cm, how much would it cost to rent a 50-cm by 50-cm by 1-m space?

A $2,500,000
B $250,000
C $5,000,000
D $50,000
E $50,000,000

6. Fiona is building a cabinet. She needs 8 pieces of trim, each 27.5 cm long. Which piece of trim would *not* be long enough for her to cut out all 8 pieces?

F a 3 m piece of trim
G a 250 cm piece of trim
H a 2,300 mm piece of trim
J a 2 m piece of trim
K Not Here

7. Which is the missing unit?

24 mm = 0.024 __?__

A mm
B cm
C m
D km

8. Which is the equivalent measure?

189 mL = __?__ L

F 0.189   **G** 1.89
H 18.9   **J** 189,000

9. Write About It Describe how you solved Problem 5.

Possible answer: I found the volume of the space in cu cm

by writing 1 m as 100 cm and multiplying 50 × 50 × 100;

I then multiplied this number of cu cm by $1 per cu cm.

Using a Glossary

Using a glossary is a good way to check your
understanding of unfamiliar terms. A **glossary** is the part
of a book that contains definitions of important words and
symbols. A glossary is usually found at the back of a
book. Read the following problem.

VOCABULARY

glossary

> Rasheed made a super soda for the class party. He
> poured 0.8 L of orange juice into a large pitcher. Then
> he added 0.4 L of seltzer water to the juice. How
> many milliliters of super soda did he make?

---

1. Look up each of the following words in the glossary at the
   back of the math book. Write a definition for each one.

   kilometer (km) _A unit for measuring length in the metric system;_
   equal to 1,000 meters.

   meter (m) _A unit for measuring length in the metric system;_
   equal to 100 centimeters.

   liter (L) _A unit for measuring capacity in the metric system;_
   equal to 1,000 mL.

   milliliter (mL) _A unit for measuring capacity in the metric system._
   There are 1,000 mL in 1 L.

   kilogram (kg) _A unit of mass in the metric system;_
   equal to 1,000 g.

   gram (g) _A unit of mass in the metric system. There are_
   _1,000 g in 1 kg._

2. Solve the problem. _0.8 L + 0.4 L = 1.2 L; 1.2 L × 1,000 =_
   1,200 mL; he made 1,200 mL of super soda.

3. What method did you use? _I used a_
   glossary to understand the meaning of the terms in the
   problem.

Use a glossary to help you. Then solve the problem.

4. Erika put her cat on a scale. She
   read that the cat had a mass of
   2,400 grams. What is the mass of
   Erika's cat in kilograms?

   _____ 2.4 kg _____

5. Tom is a long-distance swimmer.
   He swims 3.1 km each day for one
   week. How many meters does he
   swim in one week?

   _____ 21,700 m _____

Name _____

Understanding Fractions

Write the correct answer.

1. Write a fraction for the model.

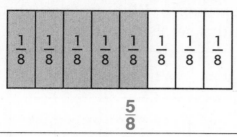

$$\frac{5}{8}$$

2. Shade the fraction strip to show $\frac{5}{6}$.

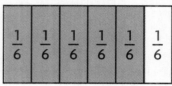

3. Judy cuts a strip of wood into 10 equal lengths. She uses 3 of the lengths. What fraction of the wood is *not* used?

$$\frac{7}{10}$$

4. Gary slices a pizza into 8 equal slices. He eats 1 of the slices. What fraction of the pizza does Gary eat?

$$\frac{1}{8}$$

Choose the letter of the correct answer.

5. Which fraction does the arrow show on the number line?

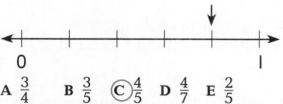

A $\frac{3}{4}$ **B** $\frac{3}{5}$ **C** $\frac{4}{5}$ **D** $\frac{4}{7}$ **E** $\frac{2}{5}$

6. Amanda's printer ribbon can print 1,200 pages. Amanda has already printed 2 reams of paper. A ream is 500 sheets. How many more pages can Amanda expect to print with the ribbon?

A 100 sheets   **B** 500 sheets
C 200 sheets   **D** 1,000 sheets

7. Cari has a dresser with 9 drawers that are all the same size. She uses 2 drawers to hold tapes and 2 drawers to hold notebooks. She uses the rest of the drawers to hold clothes. Which fraction shows the part of the dresser that holds clothes?

F $\frac{2}{9}$ **G** $\frac{4}{9}$ **H** $\frac{5}{9}$ **J** $\frac{7}{9}$

8. A singer gets royalties worth 0.01 of every dollar in record sales. His latest album earns one million dollars. How much does he earn in royalties?

F $1,000   **G** $10,000
H $100,000   **J** $1,000,000

9. Write About It Explain how you solved Problem 7.

Possible answer: 2 of the drawers hold tapes, 2 hold notebooks, so

9 - 2 - 2, or 5, hold clothes: 5 drawers out of 9 represents $\frac{5}{9}$ of the dresser.

Name _____

LESSON
15.2

Mixed Numbers

Write the correct answer.

1. Write a mixed number for the shaded part of the model.

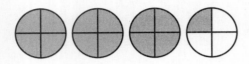

$$3\frac{1}{4}$$

2. Jim divides a piece of land for new homes. What fraction of the land is set aside for woods?

Lot 1	Lot 2	Woods	Lot 3	Lot 4
Lot 5	Woods	Woods	Woods	Lot 6

$$\frac{4}{10}, \text{ or } \frac{2}{5}$$

3. Hal breaks 1 string on his 12-string guitar. Write a fraction for the number of strings out of 12 that are unbroken.

$$\frac{11}{12}$$

4. Write the fraction $\frac{7}{2}$ as a mixed number.

$$3\frac{1}{2}$$

Choose the letter of the correct answer.

5. Which fraction is equivalent to the mixed number $4\frac{3}{8}$?

Ⓐ $\frac{35}{8}$ **B** $\frac{20}{8}$ **C** $\frac{43}{8}$ **D** $\frac{29}{8}$

6. Which mixed number is equivalent to the fraction $\frac{11}{5}$?

F $5\frac{1}{11}$ Ⓖ $2\frac{1}{5}$ **H** $1\frac{4}{5}$ **J** $1\frac{1}{5}$

7. The Jones family buys 4 pizzas. Each pizza is cut into 8 slices. They eat a total of 27 slices. Which mixed number shows how many pizzas they ate?

A $3\frac{3}{4}$ **B** $3\frac{5}{8}$ **C** $2\frac{7}{8}$

Ⓓ $3\frac{3}{8}$ **E** $2\frac{5}{8}$

8. What is the next number in the pattern?

$\frac{1}{8}, \frac{4}{8}, \frac{7}{8}, 1\frac{2}{8}, 1\frac{5}{8}, \underline{\ ?\ }$

Ⓕ 2 **G** $2\frac{1}{8}$ **H** $2\frac{3}{8}$

J $1\frac{7}{8}$ **K** Not Here

9. **Write About It** Describe the pattern you saw in Problem 8.

Possible answer: The pattern starts with $\frac{1}{8}$, then skips by $\frac{3}{8}$s,

with terms written as fractions, mixed numbers, or whole numbers.

Harcourt Brace School Publishers

Name _____

LESSON
15.4

Comparing

Write the correct answer.

1. Compare. Write $<$, $>$, or $=$ for $\bigcirc$.

$$\frac{5}{8} \bigcirc > \bigcirc \frac{9}{16}$$

2. Compare. Write $<$, $>$, or $=$ for $\bigcirc$.

$$\frac{3}{14} \bigcirc < \bigcirc \frac{2}{7}$$

3. Hot dogs come 10 in a pack. Hot dog buns come 8 in a pack. If you want to have exactly the same number of hot dogs and hot dog buns, what is the least number of packs of each you will have to buy?

_____ 4 packs of hot dogs, _____

_____ 5 packs of buns _____

4. Jack is laying out page designs for the yearbook. Six photos fit on each page. He has 22 photos to paste down. Write a mixed number for the number of pages the photos will fill.

_____

$3\frac{4}{6}$, or $3\frac{2}{3}$

Choose the letter of the correct answer.

5. Which number is the least common multiple of 8 and 18?

A 144   (B) 72   C 36   D 48

6. Which fraction is greater than $\frac{7}{9}$?

F $\frac{4}{18}$ (G) $\frac{22}{27}$ H $\frac{32}{45}$ J $\frac{2}{3}$

7. Theo is creating a menu for a dinner party. He can choose from 3 appetizers, 4 main courses, and 2 desserts. How many different meals are possible?

A 32 meals   (B) 24 meals
C 36 meals   D 12 meals
E 9 meals

8. A train travels at an average speed of 45 mile per hour. It travels 15 hours each day for 4 days. How far does the train travel during the 4-day period?

F 3,000 mi   G 4,500 mi
H 64 mi   (J) 2,700 mi
K Not Here

9. **Write About It** Explain how you can compare two fractions that have different denominators, such as the fractions in Problem 2.

Possible answer: I found the LCM of the two denominators, which

was 14, then I renamed both fractions with that denominator and

compared numerators.

Harcourt Brace School Publishers

PROBLEM SOLVING   PS77

Ordering

Write the correct answer.

1. Rename the fractions using the least common multiple as the common denominator.
$\frac{5}{9}, \frac{7}{18}, \frac{2}{3}$

   _____ $\frac{10}{18}, \frac{7}{18}, \frac{12}{18}$ _____

2. Write the fractions in order from greatest to least.
$\frac{7}{12}, \frac{5}{6}, \frac{3}{4}$

   _____ $\frac{5}{6}, \frac{3}{4}, \frac{7}{12}$ _____

3. An express bus and a local bus start out at 1st Street together. The express bus stops every 15 blocks. The local bus stops every 4 blocks. How many blocks will it be before there is a bus stop where both buses stop?

   _____ **60 blocks** _____

4. Doug and Gayle each buy a small pizza. Doug cuts his into 8 slices and eats 6 of them. Gayle cuts hers into 12 slices and eats 8 of them. Who eats more pizza?

   _____ **Doug** _____

Choose the letter of the correct answer.

5. Which group of fractions is ordered from greatest to least?

   A $\frac{2}{5}, \frac{3}{10}, \frac{7}{15}$ B $\frac{3}{10}, \frac{7}{15}, \frac{2}{5}$

   C $\frac{2}{5}, \frac{7}{15}, \frac{3}{10}$ (D) $\frac{7}{15}, \frac{2}{5}, \frac{3}{10}$

6. Which group of fractions is ordered from least to greatest?

   F $\frac{7}{9}, \frac{2}{3}, \frac{9}{12}$ G $\frac{2}{3}, \frac{7}{9}, \frac{9}{12}$

   (H) $\frac{2}{3}, \frac{9}{12}, \frac{7}{9}$ J $\frac{9}{12}, \frac{2}{3}, \frac{7}{9}$

7. Jerold buys 3 packs of markers at $3.98 each, 4 sketch pads at $2.49 each, and a charcoal pencil for $0.90. What is Jerold's total cost?

   A $7.52   (B) $22.80
   C $23.94   D $22.85

8. What digit does each symbol stand for in the following code?

   ♣♦ − ♥♠ = 42

   ♣ + ♦ + ♥ + ♠ = 19

   F ♣ = 5; ♦ = 6; ♥ = 2; ♠ = 0
   G ♣ = 5; ♦ = 7; ♥ = 1; ♠ = 6
   H ♣ = 7; ♦ = 2; ♥ = 3; ♠ = 6
   (J) ♣ = 6; ♦ = 8; ♥ = 3; ♠ = 2
   K Not Here

9. **Write About It** Explain how you ordered the fractions in Problem 6.

   <u>Possible answer: I found the LCM of the denominators—36; renamed the</u>

   <u>fractions and ordered the numerators.</u>

Observing Relationships

In a word problem it is helpful to **observe relationships**, or notice which details are related to other details. Then think about these relationships to help you solve the problem. Read the following problem.

VOCABULARY
observe
relationships

> Melva made her recipe for vegetable dip. She used $\frac{1}{3}$ cup of sour cream, $\frac{1}{6}$ cup of mustard, and $\frac{3}{4}$ cup of yogurt. She measured out each ingredient into a separate measuring cup and ordered them from greatest to least. What was the order of ingredients?

1. Underline the details in the problem. How are the details related? **The amount of each ingredient is a part of a cup and is expressed as a fraction.**

2. What do you have to do to solve this problem? **Possible answers: use fraction bars or find the least common denominator and compare.**

3. Solve the problem. $\frac{1}{3} = \frac{4}{12}; \frac{1}{6} = \frac{2}{12}; \frac{3}{4} = \frac{9}{12}.$ **The order of ingredients from greatest to least is $\frac{9}{12}$ cup yogurt, $\frac{4}{12}$ cup sour cream, $\frac{2}{12}$ cup mustard.**

4. Describe the problem-solving strategy you used. **Possible answer: I made a model with fraction bars to help me order the fractions.**

Underline the related details. Think about how they are related. Solve.

5. Ten members of the soccer team voted on where to go for a picnic. $\frac{2}{5}$ voted for Bear Lake, $\frac{1}{2}$ voted for Mead Field, and $\frac{1}{10}$ voted for the town playground. How many people voted for each location?

   Bear Lake **4**

   Mead Field **5**

   town playground **1**

6. There are 12 students with clown wigs in the play: $\frac{1}{6}$ wear orange wigs, $\frac{1}{2}$ wear blue wigs, $\frac{1}{4}$ wear green wigs, and $\frac{1}{12}$ wear red wigs. What is the order of the colors of wigs from least to greatest?

   red, orange, green, blue

Greatest Common Factor

Write the correct answer.

1. List the factors of the number 36.

   _____ 1, 2, 3, 4, 6, 9, 12, 18, 36 _____

2. Write the greatest common factor for the numbers 16 and 44.

   _____ 4 _____

3. Ty is packaging homemade candles to sell. In each box of 12 candles, he includes 3 green, 3 red, 3 white, 2 silver, and 1 gold. What fraction of the candles in each box are gold?

   $\frac{1}{12}$

4. Fernando sprinkles $6\frac{1}{2}$ pounds of plant food on his rose garden. Write the mixed number $6\frac{1}{2}$ as a fraction.

   $\frac{13}{2}$

Choose the letter of the correct answer.

5. Which number is the greatest common factor of 15 and 60?

   A 2   **B** 3   **C** 5   **(D)** 15

6. Which number is *not* a factor of 48?

   F 6   **G** 8   **H** 12   **(J)** 36

7. Mac is tiling a new bathroom. He starts at the corner of the shower stall and puts a row of 8-in. wide tiles near the floor. Above this row, starting at the same corner, he puts a row of 3-in. wide tiles. How far from the corner will Mac have to go before the tiles in the two rows line up again?

   A 12 in.
   B 8 in.
   C 48 in.
   (D) 24 in.
   E Not Here

8. Shelly and Laura go to the starting line of a circular $\frac{1}{4}$-mile running track together. Shelly stays at the starting line to stretch. Laura runs $\frac{1}{2}$ mile. When Laura finishes her run, how far is she from Shelly?

   F 2 mi
   G $\frac{1}{2}$ mi
   H $\frac{3}{4}$ mi
   (J) next to her
   K 1 mi

9. **Write About It** Explain how you solved Problem 8.

   Possible answer: I drew a picture. Both girls start at the

   starting line. Shelly stays there. After $\frac{1}{2}$ mile, or two

   laps, Laura ends up back where she started, next to Shelly.

Equivalent Fractions

Write the correct answer.

1. Use multiplication or division to write a fraction equivalent to $\frac{4}{10}$.

Possible answer: $\frac{2}{5}$

2. Use multiplication or division to write a fraction equivalent to $\frac{3}{16}$.

Possible answer: $\frac{6}{32}$

3. Patrick has three pieces of wire. They are $\frac{7}{10}$ m, $\frac{3}{5}$ m, and $\frac{11}{20}$ m in length. Which piece is longest?

$\frac{7}{10}$ m

4. Lizzy gets her paycheck every 10 days. Her husband, Don, gets a paycheck every 14 days. On July 3, they both get a paycheck. How many days will pass before they both get a paycheck on the same day again?

70 days

Choose the letter of the correct answer.

5. Which fraction is *not* equivalent to $\frac{2}{3}$?

A $\frac{4}{6}$ B $\frac{16}{24}$ C $\frac{20}{30}$ (D) $\frac{9}{12}$

6. Which number is *not* a factor of 42?

F 2   (G) 4   H 6   J 21

7. Sammy works in a grocery store. He wants to set up a display of almonds in a large box. Which of the boxes below will hold the greatest number of almonds?

A 6 in. × 8 in. × 12 in.
B 8 in. × 9 in. × 9 in.
C 7 in. × 10 in. × 10 in.
D 14 in. × 6 in. × 6 in.
(E) 10 in. × 9 in. × 8 in.

8. Yolanda has two grandfather clocks in her home. One must be wound every 6 days. The other must be wound every 14 days. Yolanda winds up both clocks on December 15. When is the next time she will have to wind both of the clocks on the same day?

F December 29   G January 31
(H) January 26   J February 3
K Not Here

9. **Write About It** Explain how you solved Problem 8.

Possible answer: I found the greatest common factor of 6 and 14, which is 42; 42 days is exactly 6 weeks, so I skip counted 6 weeks from Dec. 15 on my calendar.

Comparing and Contrasting

When you **compare** two or more things, you look at how they are alike. When you **contrast** two or more things, you look at how they are different. Read the following problem.

VOCABULARY
compare
contrast

Alex saved $16.00 in one month. He saved $\frac{1}{8}$ of the money the first week, $\frac{1}{2}$ of the money the second week, $\frac{2}{16}$ of the money the third week, and $\frac{1}{4}$ of the money the last week. During which week did he save the most money?

1. Compare and contrast different parts of the problem. Complete the chart.

ALIKE	DIFFERENT
Alex saves money every week for 4 weeks.	He saves a different amount of money each week.
The information about how much he saves each week is given in fractions.	Each fraction has a different denominator.

2. Solve the problem. **Compare the fractions. $\frac{1}{2} > \frac{1}{4} > \frac{2}{16}$, or $\frac{1}{8}$. So, he saved the most money during the second week.**

3. Describe the problem-solving strategy you used. **Possible answer: I drew a diagram of a number line to compare the fractional amounts.**

Use a chart to compare and contrast. Solve.

4. Hannah sorted the 18 tomatoes she picked. Of the tomatoes, $\frac{1}{6}$ were red, $\frac{1}{3}$ were yellow, and $\frac{1}{2}$ were green. What color tomatoes did she pick most of? the least of?

_____ green; red _____

5. Craig has 24 pairs of socks. He has an equal number of striped pairs, colored pairs, and white pairs. Write two equivalent fractions to describe the fraction of the pairs of socks that are striped.

_____ $\frac{8}{24}, \frac{1}{3}$ _____

Simplest Form

Write the correct answer.

1. Use the fraction bars to help you write the fraction $\frac{6}{10}$ in simplest form.

$\frac{1}{10}$	$\frac{1}{10}$	$\frac{1}{10}$	$\frac{1}{10}$	$\frac{1}{10}$	$\frac{1}{10}$
$\frac{1}{5}$		$\frac{1}{5}$		$\frac{1}{5}$	

$$\frac{3}{5}$$
_____

2. Write the fraction $\frac{6}{12}$ in simplest form. You may use fraction bars.

$$\frac{1}{2}$$
_____

3. Out of a class of 24 students, 10 are girls. Write an equivalent fraction to show the part of the class that is girls.

Possible answer: $\frac{5}{12}$
_____

4. Dale is second-string quarterback on the school football team this year. He kept track of the number of quarters he played during the season—a total of 17 quarters. Write as a mixed number the total number of games he played.

$4\frac{1}{4}$ games

Choose the letter of the correct answer.

5. Which fraction is the simplest form of $\frac{12}{15}$?

A $\frac{12}{15}$ B $\frac{3}{5}$ Ⓒ $\frac{4}{5}$ D $\frac{6}{10}$ E $\frac{2}{5}$

6. Which fraction is the simplest form of $\frac{10}{21}$?

F $\frac{5}{10}$ G $\frac{7}{15}$ Ⓗ $\frac{10}{21}$ J $\frac{21}{10}$

7. Fred tears an $8\frac{1}{2}$-in. by 11-in. sheet of paper into 11 strips. What is the average area of a strip?

Ⓐ $8\frac{1}{2}$ sq in.   B $4\frac{1}{4}$ sq in.
C $93\frac{1}{2}$ sq in.   D 1 sq in.
E Not Here

8. Jackie's car travels 340 miles on 8.5 gallons of gasoline. If gas costs $1.39 per gallon, which number sentence can you use to find the cost for 1 mile's worth of gas?

Ⓕ $1.39 ÷ (340 ÷ 8.5)
G $1.39 × (340 ÷ 8.5)
H (340 ÷ 8.5) ÷ $1.39
J $1.39 ÷ 8.5 × 340

9. **Write About It** Explain the reasoning you used in solving Problem 7.

Possible answer: The average area is equal to the total area divided by
the number of pieces; the area = $8\frac{1}{2}$ × 11, so the average area = $8\frac{1}{2}$ × 11
divided by 11.

More About Simplest Form

Write the correct answer.

1. Write the fraction $\frac{8}{24}$ in simplest form.

$$\frac{1}{3}$$

2. Write the fraction $\frac{11}{32}$ in simplest form.

$$\frac{11}{32}$$

3. Of the 50 states in the United States, 5 have Pacific Ocean coastlines. Write a fraction in simplest form that shows what fraction of the states have Pacific Ocean coastlines.

$$\frac{1}{10}$$

4. The Carter family spends $\frac{2}{9}$ of its budget on rent, $\frac{1}{3}$ of its budget on child care, and $\frac{1}{6}$ of its budget on insurance. Order the items in the Carter budget from least amount spent to greatest amount spent.

insurance, rent, child care

Choose the letter of the correct answer.

5. Which is the simplest form for the fraction $\frac{6}{36}$?

(A) $\frac{1}{6}$　　**B** $\frac{1}{3}$　　**C** $\frac{4}{9}$　　**D** $\frac{2}{12}$

6. Which fraction is *not* equivalent to $\frac{7}{8}$?

F $\frac{14}{16}$　　(G) $\frac{35}{48}$

H $\frac{49}{56}$　　**J** $\frac{42}{48}$

7. Four of the planets have a smaller volume than Earth's. Here are the fractions of Earth's volume for these planets: Mercury: $\frac{1}{18}$; Venus: $\frac{17}{20}$; Mars: $\frac{3}{20}$; Pluto: $\frac{1}{100}$. Which choice below lists these four planets from least volume to greatest volume?

A Mercury, Venus, Pluto, Mars
B Venus, Pluto, Mars, Mercury
(C) Pluto, Mercury, Mars, Venus
D Pluto, Mars, Mercury, Venus
E Venus, Mars, Mercury, Pluto

8. Victor is playing a game in which he moves a piece on a chessboard. He moves his piece 4 squares forward, 3 squares to the right, 2 squares right, 2 squares forward, 4 squares back, 1 square left, and 1 square back. Which of the moves below will get Victor's piece back to the square it started on?

F 4 back, 2 left　　**G** 4 left, 2 back
H 4 left, 3 back　　**J** 2 back, 3 left
(K) Not Here

9. Write About It Describe the method you used to solve Problem 8.

Possible answer: I used a piece of grid paper and acted it out, making

each move, then trying out the combinations in the answer choices.

Adding Like Fractions

Write the correct answer.

1. Use the fraction strips to find the sum $\frac{1}{5} + \frac{3}{5}$.

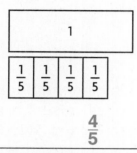

$\frac{4}{5}$

2. Use the fraction strips to find the sum $\frac{5}{6} + \frac{3}{6}$. Write the sum in simplest form.

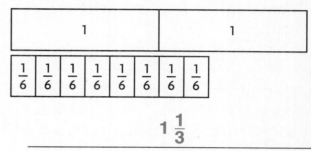

$1\frac{1}{3}$

3. Charlie bakes an apple pie and slices it into 12 equal slices. His family eats 8 of the slices. Write a fraction in simplest form for the part of the pie they ate.

$\frac{2}{3}$ of the pie

4. Elena has 12 floor tiles she wants to arrange in a rectangular pattern in the center of her kitchen floor. Write all of the dimensions of the rectangles she could make with the tiles.

Possible answers:
$1 \times 12, 2 \times 6, 3 \times 4$

Choose the letter of the correct answer.

5. What is the sum of $\frac{3}{8} + \frac{7}{8}$ written in simplest form?

A $\frac{10}{8}$ B $1\frac{2}{8}$ Ⓒ $1\frac{1}{4}$ D $\frac{10}{16}$

6. What is the sum of $\frac{4}{9} + \frac{4}{9}$ written in simplest form?

F $\frac{8}{18}$ G $\frac{4}{9}$ H $1\frac{1}{8}$ Ⓙ $\frac{8}{9}$

7. Aaron and Pete built a model railroad with pieces of track that are 9 in. long. Which of the following can not be the total length of track they used?

A 12 ft, 9 in.   B 8 ft, 3 in.
C 15 ft   D 9 ft
Ⓔ 5 ft, 6 in.

8. Barbara makes a pan of brownies and wants to cut them into 24 equal pieces. Which of the following ways of cutting the brownies will *not* give 24 pieces?

F 2 pieces wide by 12 pieces long
G 3 pieces wide by 8 pieces long
H 4 pieces wide by 6 pieces long
J 1 piece wide by 24 pieces long
Ⓚ Not Here

9. **Write About It** Describe the method you used to solve Problem 7.

Possible answer: The total track length must be a multiple of 9 in.,

so I tested each answer choice by renaming it using inches.

Using the Least Common Denominator
to Add Fractions

Write the correct answer.

1. Use the least common multiple to name the least common denominator for the fractions $\frac{3}{8}$ and $\frac{5}{12}$.

_____ 24 _____

2. Write the sum in simplest form.
$\frac{3}{4} + \frac{3}{8} = \underline{\ ?\ }$

$1\frac{1}{8}$
_____

3. Carl buys $\frac{3}{4}$ pound of sliced ham, $\frac{7}{8}$ pound of bologna, and $\frac{1}{2}$ pound of sliced turkey. Which meat does he buy the most of?

_____ bologna _____

_____

4. Cans of juice come in packages of 8 cans. Boxes of raisins come in packages of 6 boxes. What is the least number of packages you could buy so that you had the same number of raisin boxes as cans of juice?

___ 3 packages of juice and ___

___ 4 packages of raisins ___

Choose the letter of the correct answer.

5. What is the sum in simplest form?
$\frac{9}{15} + \frac{2}{5} = \underline{\ ?\ }$
A $\frac{11}{20}$ B $\frac{13}{15}$ C⃝ 1   D $1\frac{1}{15}$

6. What is the sum in simplest form?
$\frac{8}{9} + \frac{2}{3} = \underline{\ ?\ }$
F $\frac{14}{9}$ G $\frac{10}{12}$ H $\frac{5}{6}$ J⃝ $1\frac{5}{9}$

7. Tim is building a bridge. He has 3 pieces like the one shown. He attaches the three to form one long piece. What is the total length of the long piece?

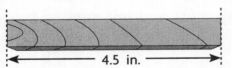

← 4.5 in. →

A 12 in.   B 19 in.   C⃝ 13.5 in.
D 11.5 in.   E 13 in.

8. Meg spends 3 hours 20 minutes loading new software on her computer. Then she spends 1 hour 50 minutes trying out the new software. At 4:15 P.M., she shuts down her computer. At what time did she start loading the software?

F 12:55 A.M.   G 12:55 P.M.
H⃝ 11:05 A.M.   J 2:25 P.M.
K Not Here

9. **Write About It** Explain how you solved Problem 7.

   I multiplied the length, 4.5 in., by 3, giving a product of 13.5 in.
_____

Adding Three Fractions

Write the correct answer.

1. Use the least common multiple, (LCM) to name the least common denominator, (LCD) of the fractions
$\frac{3}{8}, \frac{5}{16}, \frac{1}{2}.$

_____16_____

2. Write the sum in simplest form.
$\frac{5}{12} + \frac{1}{3} + \frac{3}{4} = \frac{?}{}$

$1\frac{1}{2}$

3. Monica and Howard bake a pizza. Monica says she wants $\frac{1}{4}$ of it, and Howard says he wants $\frac{1}{3}$. What is the smallest number of equal pieces they can slice so that they can each get the fraction they want?

_____12 pieces_____

4. Rena glues a $\frac{1}{2}$-in.-thick piece of wood to a $\frac{3}{8}$-in.-thick piece of wood. How thick is the glued piece?

$\frac{7}{8}$ in. thick

Choose the letter of the correct answer.

5. Which fraction shows the amount of the budget spent on team support, insurance, and uniforms?

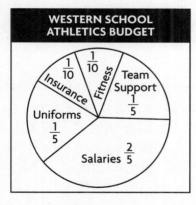

WESTERN SCHOOL ATHLETICS BUDGET
Insurance $\frac{1}{10}$
Fitness $\frac{1}{10}$
Team Support $\frac{1}{5}$
Uniforms $\frac{1}{5}$
Salaries $\frac{2}{5}$

A $\frac{4}{31}$ B $\frac{1}{2}$ C $\frac{5}{15}$ D $\frac{3}{10}$

6. Use the circle graph in Problem 5. What is the least common denominator for the group of fractions used in the circle graph?

F 10   G 24   H 15   J 60

7. A cookie recipe calls for $\frac{3}{4}$ cup whole wheat flour, $\frac{2}{3}$ cup cake flour, and $\frac{1}{2}$ cup soy flour. It also calls for $\frac{3}{4}$ cup sugar. What is the total measure of these ingredients?

F 2 c   G $1\frac{3}{4}$ c   H $2\frac{2}{3}$ c
J $3\frac{1}{3}$ c   K Not Here

8. **Write About It** Explain how you solved Problem 7.

Possible answer: $\frac{3}{4} + \frac{2}{3} + \frac{1}{2} + \frac{3}{4}$. 12 is the LCD; so $\frac{9}{12} + \frac{8}{12} + \frac{6}{12} + \frac{9}{12} = \frac{32}{12}$, or $2\frac{2}{3}$ c.

Making Inferences

You can make logical connections, or **inferences,** to help you solve a problem. The factual information often gives clues about the unstated information in the problem. Read the following problem.

> All the girls in the fifth-grade class at Wasichu School voted in the election for class treasurer. Of the girls, $\frac{1}{2}$ voted for Alice and $\frac{1}{8}$ voted for Joe. What fraction of the girls voted for other candidates?

VOCABULARY
inferences

1. Examine the information from the problem in the table.
2. Look at the factual information and make inferences. Write your inferences in the table next to the factual information.

Factual Information	Inferences
All the girls voted.	**Possible answer: All the fractions, including the answer, will add up to 1.**
$\frac{1}{2}$ of the girls voted for Alice. $\frac{1}{8}$ of the girls voted for Joe.	**Possible answer: $\frac{5}{8}$ of the girls voted for Alice or Joe.**

3. Solve the problem. $1 - \frac{5}{8} = \frac{3}{8}$; $\frac{3}{8}$ **of the girls voted for other candidates.**

4. Describe the problem-solving strategy you used. **Possible answer: I made a model with fraction bars.**

Make inferences. Solve.

5. Alan has 19 plants in his garden. He has a row of 4 cabbages, a row of 12 carrots, and a row of 3 bean plants. The bean plants are in the back. The cabbages are behind the carrots. Which plants are in front?

   Inference: The garden has only

   3 rows of plants. Answer:

   The carrots are in front.

6. Maya spent 1 hour doing math, social studies, and science homework. She spent $\frac{1}{3}$ of the time on math and $\frac{1}{2}$ of the time on science. How long did Maya spend on social studies?

   Inference: Maya spent $\frac{1}{3} + \frac{1}{2}$, or $\frac{5}{6}$ of

   the hour doing math and science.

   So, $\frac{1}{6}$ of the time was spent on social

   studies. Possible answer: If 60 minutes is divided into 6 equal parts, $\frac{1}{6}$ hour equals 10 min. So, Maya spent 10 min on social studies.

Subtracting Like Fractions

Write the correct answer.

1. Write the difference in simplest form.

   $\frac{5}{8} - \frac{3}{8} = $ ____?

   _____ $\frac{1}{4}$ _____

2. Write the difference in simplest form.

   $\frac{7}{9} - \frac{5}{9} = $ ____?

   _____ $\frac{2}{9}$ _____

3. Karen asks her aunt how old she is. "My age is a prime number," her aunt tells her. "I am older than 47 and younger than 59. How old is Karen's aunt?

   _____ **53 years old** _____

4. Lloyd is thinking of a number. "It's an odd number less than 100 and it is a multiple of 5 and of 7," Lloyd says. What is his number?

   _____ **35** _____

Choose the letter of the correct answer.

5. What is the difference in simplest form?

   $\frac{7}{10} - \frac{3}{10} = $ ____?

   A $\frac{4}{10}$ **B** $\frac{3}{5}$ **C** $\frac{2}{5}$ **D** 1

7. Wanda is scheduled to work Monday through Friday from 9:00 A.M. to 5:00 P.M. One week, she arrives at 8:52 A.M. and leaves at 5:08 P.M. every day. How many extra minutes does she work that week?

   A 70 min
   B 80 min
   C 65 min
   D 150 min
   E 230 min

6. What is the sum in simplest form?

   $\frac{1}{2} + \frac{3}{5} + \frac{7}{10} = $ ____?

   F $\frac{9}{5}$ **G** $\frac{18}{10}$ **H** $\frac{11}{17}$ **J** $1\frac{4}{5}$

8. A class of 66 students visited an art museum. A third of them visited the sculpture garden. One half of that number went to the Impressionist exhibit. The remaining students visited the Egyptian gallery. How many students visited the Egyptian gallery?

   F 44 students
   G 48 students
   H 16 students
   J 33 students
   K Not Here

9. **Write About It** Explain how you solved Problem 3.

   **Possible answer: 53 is the only prime number between 47 and 59; its only**

   **factors are 1 and 53.**

Using the Least Common Denominator to Subtract Fractions

Write the correct answer.

1. Write the difference in simplest form.

$$\frac{7}{8} - \frac{1}{4} = \underline{\ ?\ }$$

$$\frac{5}{8}$$

2. Write the difference in simplest form.

$$\frac{1}{3} - \frac{2}{9} = \underline{\ ?\ }$$

$$\frac{1}{9}$$

3. Sheryl mows $\frac{1}{2}$ of her yard on Tuesday, $\frac{1}{4}$ of it on Wednesday, and $\frac{1}{8}$ on Thursday. She finishes it on Friday. What part of the yard does she mow on Friday?

$$\frac{1}{8}$$

4. Tina spends $\frac{1}{4}$ of her paycheck each month on rent, $\frac{3}{10}$ of it on health insurance, and $\frac{1}{5}$ of it on tuition. Which expense is greatest?

health insurance

Choose the letter of the correct answer.

5. What is the difference in simplest form?

$$\frac{9}{12} - \frac{1}{2} = \underline{\ ?\ }$$

(A) $\frac{1}{4}$ B $\frac{5}{12}$ C $\frac{1}{3}$ D $\frac{1}{6}$

6. What is the sum in simplest form?

$$\frac{5}{9} + \frac{1}{3} + \frac{2}{9} = \underline{\ ?\ }$$

F $2\frac{1}{9}$ G $\frac{11}{9}$ (H) $1\frac{1}{9}$ J $1\frac{1}{7}$

7. Sven borrows $2,500. The bank charges him an additional 0.05 of his loan in interest. How much interest will he owe?

A $166.67
B $210.00
C $187.50
D $250.00
(E) $125.00

8. Beth builds a square pyramid out of blocks. The top layer has 1 block, the next layer down has 4 blocks, the next has 9 blocks, and the next has 16 blocks. How many blocks are in the next layer?

F 20
G 30
H 35
(J) 25
K Not Here

9. **Write About It** Describe the pattern you used to solve Problem 8.

Possible answer: Each layer is a square: 1 × 1, 2 × 2, 3 × 3, 4 × 4, so the

next layer is 5 × 5, or 25.

Subtracting Fractions Using a Ruler

Write the correct answer.

1. Use the ruler to help you find the difference.

$\frac{7}{8}$ in. $-\frac{1}{4}$ in. = __?__

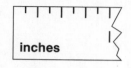

inches

_____ $\frac{5}{8}$ in. _____

2. Use the ruler to help you find the difference.

$\frac{3}{4}$ in. $-\frac{5}{8}$ in. = __?__

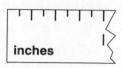

inches

_____ $\frac{1}{8}$ in. _____

3. The track at Bill's school is $\frac{3}{4}$ mile long. The track at Vernon's school is $\frac{2}{3}$ mile long. Which school has the longer track?

_____ **Bill's school** _____

4. Jack's drive to work is $\frac{9}{10}$ mile. His drive to his brother's house is $\frac{1}{2}$ mile. How much longer is his drive to work?

_____ $\frac{4}{10}$, or $\frac{2}{5}$, mile _____

Choose the letter of the correct answer.

5. $\frac{11}{16}$ in. $-\frac{5}{8}$ in. = __?__

    A $\frac{6}{8}$ in.　　　　B $\frac{3}{4}$ in.

    C $\frac{1}{8}$ in.　　　　(D) $\frac{1}{16}$ in.

6. $\frac{1}{2}$ in. $-\frac{1}{16}$ in. = __?__

    F $\frac{3}{16}$ in.　　　　(G) $\frac{7}{16}$ in.

    H $\frac{1}{8}$ in.　　　　J $\frac{5}{16}$ in.

7. What is the most reasonable estimate of this CD's total playing time?

CD Playing Time				
Track	1	2	3	4
Min:sec	16:32	7:41	21:19	10:11

(A) 56 min　　B 58 min　　C 54 min
D 62 min　　E 66 min

8. Julie pulls a marble out of a bag of 3 blue marbles, 2 red marbles, and 5 yellow marbles. What is the probability that she will pull out a red marble?

    F $\frac{2}{5}$　　　　　　G $\frac{1}{2}$

    H $\frac{3}{10}$　　　　　(J) $\frac{1}{5}$

    K Not Here

9. **Write About It** Explain how you solved Problem 8.

    There are 10 marbles in the bag. The red marbles make up 2 out of the 10.

    This gives the probability of $\frac{2}{10}$, or $\frac{1}{5}$ in simplest form.

Name _____

Understanding Cause and Effect

Sometimes information in a problem is related. One detail affects another. The **cause** is the reason something happens. The **effect** is the result. Read the following problem.

VOCABULARY
cause
effect

> The directions for Jim's stalactite kit tell the grower that at a temperature of 45° the stalactites will grow 1.5 in. a day. At a temperature of 50° the stalactites will grow 2.0 inches a day, and at 55° they will grow 2.5 in. a day. How much will the stalactites grow a day at 65°?

1. Use the information in the problem above to complete the cause-and-effect chart.

CAUSE	EFFECT
The temperature is 45°.	The stalactites grow 1.5 in. a day.
The temperature is 50°.	The stalactites grow 2.0 in. a day.
The temperature is 55°.	The stalactites grow 2.5 in. a day.

2. What pattern do you see in the cause-and-effect chart for the problem? __With every 5° increase in temperature, the stalactites grow 0.5 in.__

3. Solve the problem. __At 65° the stalactites will grow 3.5 in. a day.__

4. Describe the strategy you used. __I found a pattern in the increased temperature and increased growth.__

Look for the cause-and-effect relationships. Solve.

5. A bank has different interest rates for its accounts. Deposits from $1 to $500, earn 0.03 on each dollar; up to $1,000, 0.04 on each dollar; to $1,500, 0.05 on each dollar. If Mickey deposits $760 in an account, how much money will be in the account after one year?

__$790.40__

6. Dane is a sculptor. It takes him about 3 days to carve a piece of wood that is 4 cu ft, 6 days for 8 cu ft, and 12 days for 16 cu ft. Dane will carve a piece that is 32 cu ft. About how many days will it take him to carve this sculpture?

__24 days__

Name _____

Estimating Sums and Differences

Write the correct answer.

1. Write whether the fraction $\frac{6}{10}$ is closer to 0, $\frac{1}{2}$, or 1.

_____ **$\frac{1}{2}$** _____

2. Write whether the fraction $\frac{7}{8}$ is closer to 0, $\frac{1}{2}$, or 1.

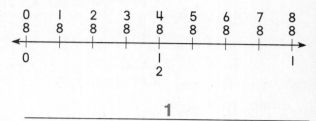

_____ **1** _____

3. Write whether the fraction $\frac{3}{16}$ is closer to 0, $\frac{1}{2}$, or 1.

_____ **0** _____

4. Write whether the fraction $\frac{5}{12}$ is closer to 0, $\frac{1}{2}$, or 1.

_____ **$\frac{1}{2}$** _____

Choose the letter of the correct answer.

5. What is the most reasonable estimate?

$\frac{5}{8} - \frac{1}{5} = $ ___?

A 0   **(B)** $\frac{1}{2}$ **C** 1   **D** $1\frac{1}{2}$

6. What is the most reasonable estimate?

$\frac{9}{11} + \frac{3}{5} = $ ___?

F 0   **G** $\frac{1}{2}$ **H** 1   **(J)** $1\frac{1}{2}$

7. An octave on a piano keyboard has 5 black keys and 7 white keys. How many more white keys than black keys are in six octaves on a piano keyboard?

A 6
B 2
C 72
D 88
(E) 12

8. The number Φ is twice the number Σ. Which of the following is reasonable to say about the fraction $\frac{\Sigma}{\Phi}$?

F It is equal to 1.
G It is equal to 1.
(H) It is equal to $\frac{1}{2}$.
J It is equal to 0.
K Not Here

9. **Write About It**   Describe how you solved Problem 7.

Possible answer: In 6 octaves, there are 5 × 6, or 30,

black keys and 7 × 6, or 42, white keys: 42 − 30 = 12.

Adding and Subtracting Like Fractions

Write the correct answer.

1. Write the sum in simplest form.

$$\frac{3}{10} + \frac{9}{10} = \underline{\quad?\quad}$$

$$1\frac{1}{5}$$

2. Write the difference in simplest form.

$$\frac{11}{12} - \frac{3}{12} = \underline{\quad?\quad}$$

$$\frac{2}{3}$$

3. Write whether the fraction $\frac{9}{16}$ is closer to 0, $\frac{1}{2}$, or 1.

$$\frac{1}{2}$$

4. Write whether the fraction $\frac{2}{9}$ is closer to 0, $\frac{1}{2}$, or 1.

$$0$$

Choose the letter of the correct answer.

5. What is the difference in simplest form?

$$\frac{4}{5} - \frac{1}{5} = \underline{\quad?\quad}$$

A 3   (B) $\frac{3}{5}$ C $\frac{6}{10}$ D $\frac{2}{5}$

6. What is the sum in simplest form?

$$\frac{2}{9} + \frac{7}{9} = \underline{\quad?\quad}$$

F $\frac{8}{9}$ G $\frac{9}{18}$ H $\frac{2}{9}$ (J) 1

7. Jerry's Print Shop rents computer time for \$2 for $\frac{1}{6}$ hour. Dana rents a computer for $\frac{3}{6}$ hour on Wednesday and for $\frac{2}{6}$ hour on Thursday. She pays for the rental using a \$10 bill. How much change should she receive?

A \$2   B \$4   C \$1
(D) \$0   E \$5

8. A sauce recipe says to "reduce sauce by half." This means to cook it until $\frac{1}{2}$ of it has boiled away. The recipe for 1 cup of finished sauce calls for $\frac{3}{4}$ cup lemon juice and $1\frac{1}{4}$ cup fish stock. Rosalie wants 2 cups of finished sauce. How much fish stock does she need to start with?

F 3 cups   G $\frac{3}{4}$ cups
(H) $2\frac{1}{2}$ cups   J $1\frac{1}{2}$ cups
K Not Here

9. **Write About It** Describe all of the steps you took to solve Problem 2.

<u>Possible answer: First, I compared denominators; they were alike, so I</u>

<u>subtracted numerators and wrote the difference over the denominator:</u>

<u>$\frac{8}{12}$. I simplified by dividing numerator and denominator by the GCF of 4:</u>

<u>$\frac{8}{12} = \frac{2}{3}$.</u>

Adding and Subtracting Unlike Fractions

Write the correct answer.

1. Write the difference $\frac{5}{6} - \frac{1}{3}$ in simplest form.

$$\frac{1}{2}$$

2. Write the sum $\frac{5}{8} + \frac{7}{16}$ in simplest form.

$$1\frac{1}{16}$$

3. Vic covers $\frac{8}{9}$ of a kitchen floor with tiles. White tiles cover $\frac{5}{9}$ of the floor. The rest of the tiled part is covered with black tiles. What part of the floor is covered with black tiles?

$$\frac{3}{9}, \text{ or } \frac{1}{3}$$

4. Of the 12 students in Marie's class, 11 of them dislike anchovies on pizza. Write whether the fraction $\frac{11}{12}$ is closer to 0, $\frac{1}{2}$, or 1.

$$1$$

Choose the letter of the correct answer.

5. What is the sum in simplest form?

$$\frac{6}{7} + \frac{1}{2} = \underline{\ ?\ }$$

A 2   **B** $\frac{17}{14}$ **C** $\frac{7}{9}$ **D** $1\frac{5}{14}$

6. What is the most reasonable estimate of the sum?

$$\frac{1}{5} + \frac{3}{8} = \underline{\ ?\ }$$

F 0   **G** $\frac{1}{2}$ **H** 1   **J** $1\frac{1}{2}$

7. Cheetahs can run at speeds of up to 70 miles per hour. Sound waves travel about 10 times as fast. Which of the following is a reasonable conclusion ?

A Sound travels at about 7 mph.
B Sound travels at about 700 mph.
C Sound takes about 10 times as long as a cheetah to move the same distance.
D Cheetahs run about as fast as the speed of sound.
E Not Here

8. When two number cubes are rolled together, the probability of rolling a sum of 4 is $\frac{3}{36}$. Which choice best describes the chances of rolling a sum of 4 when you roll two number cubes?

F about as likely as not
G unlikely
H very likely
J impossible
K certain

9. **Write About It** Write a sentence to describe what part of Marie's class in Problem 4 likes anchovies on pizza. Use words such as *almost all*, *only a few*, or *about half*.

Possible answer: Only a few of the students in Marie's

class like anchovies.

Practicing Addition and Subtraction

Write the correct answer.

1. Write the sum in simplest form.

   $\frac{6}{7} + \frac{9}{14} = $ __?__

   _____
   $1\frac{1}{2}$

2. Write the difference in simplest form.

   $1\frac{1}{12} - \frac{2}{3} = $ __?__

   _____
   $\frac{5}{12}$

3. Mark ate $\frac{7}{12}$ of a pizza for lunch and $\frac{7}{8}$ of a pizza for dinner. Estimate the total amount of pizza Mark ate.

   _____
   $1\frac{1}{2}$ pizzas

4. Dennis played 3 quarters of the first basketball game and 2 quarters of the second. How much did he play in all during the two games?

   _____
   $1\frac{1}{4}$ games

Choose the letter of the correct answer.

5. What is the sum in simplest form?

   $\frac{9}{15} + \frac{3}{5} = $ __?__

   A $\frac{18}{15}$ **B** $1\frac{3}{15}$ Ⓒ $1\frac{1}{5}$ **D** $\frac{3}{5}$

6. What is the difference in simplest form?

   $\frac{9}{12} - \frac{1}{2} = $ __?__

   Ⓕ $\frac{1}{4}$ **G** $\frac{5}{12}$ **H** $1\frac{3}{12}$ **J** $\frac{1}{12}$

7. During last April in Appleton, it rained an average of 0.12 in. every day of the month. Appleton's normal total rainfall for the month of April is 2.1 in. How much more rainfall did Appleton get last April than during an average April?

   Ⓐ 1.5 in.
   B 3.6 in.
   C 1.62 in.
   D 3.72 in.
   E 2.98 in.

8. Physicists measure parts of atoms using *electron volts*. A mega-electron volt, or MeV, is 1 million electron volts. A tera-electron volt, or TeV, is 1 trillion electron volts. A giga-electron volt, or GeV, is 1 billion electron volts. Which choice shows these masses from least to greatest?

   F GeV, TeV, MeV
   G TeV, GeV, MeV
   H MeV, TeV, GeV
   Ⓙ MeV, GeV, TeV
   K Not Here

9. **Write About It** Describe how you solved Problem 7.

   Possible answer: I multiplied 0.12 per day × 30 days in April, then
   _____

   subtracted 2.1 from the product. 3.6 − 2.1 = 1.5
   _____

Choosing Addition or Subtraction

Write the correct answer.

1. Janis brings $\frac{3}{4}$ of a sandwich for lunch. She gives $\frac{1}{4}$ of the sandwich to a friend. Which operation would you use to calculate what fraction of a sandwich Janis has left?

_____subtraction_____

2. Amanda's chocolate-chip cookie recipe calls for $\frac{7}{8}$ cup brown sugar and $\frac{1}{4}$ cup white sugar. Which operation would you use to calculate how much more brown sugar than white sugar is needed?

_____subtraction_____

3. Nate jogs $\frac{1}{2}$ mile to the park and then $\frac{9}{10}$ mile on the park running track. How far does Nate jog in all?

$1\frac{4}{10}$, or $1\frac{2}{5}$, miles

4. Mickey makes $\frac{3}{4}$ pint of strawberry ice cream and $\frac{3}{4}$ pint of blueberry-vanilla ice cream. Does he make more than 1 pint of ice cream in all?

_____yes_____

Choose the letter of the correct answer.

5. Of the fifth-grade students, $\frac{1}{5}$ play in the school band. Another $\frac{3}{7}$ play some instrument but *not* in the school band. Which operation would you use to calculate the fraction of the class that plays an instrument?

(A) addition   B subtraction
C multiplication   D division

6. Jill conducts a survey. Of the people interviewed, $\frac{2}{5}$ think their senator is doing a good job. Another $\frac{2}{5}$ think their senator is *not* doing a good job. The remaining people have no opinion. What fraction of the people interviewed have no opinion?

(F) $\frac{1}{5}$ G $\frac{2}{5}$ H $\frac{3}{5}$ J $\frac{1}{10}$

7. Which number comes next in the pattern?

2, 3, 5, 7, 11, 13, 17, 19, 23, __?__

A 25   B 27   C 28
(D) 29   E 31

8. Sales tax is $0.06 for every dollar spent. Caitlin buys a coat and pays $7.32 in sales tax. Which price would be a reasonable estimate of how much the coat cost?

F $15   G $50   H $1,400
(J) $120   K Not Here

9. **Write About It** Describe the pattern you saw in Problem 7.

Possible answer: The numbers in the pattern are the prime numbers.

Understanding Multistep Problems

Sometimes you need to use two or more steps to solve a
problem. As you read, think about how many steps you
will use to solve the following problem.

> Jorge's class conducted a survey to find out which
> activity students preferred. Of the class, $\frac{1}{10}$ chose
> playing video games, $\frac{3}{10}$ chose watching television,
> and $\frac{3}{5}$ chose going on-line on the Internet. If there are
> 30 students in Jorge's class, how many more students
> chose going on-line than chose watching television?

1. Draw a number line to model the problem. The whole number
   line represents the total number of students in Jorge's class.

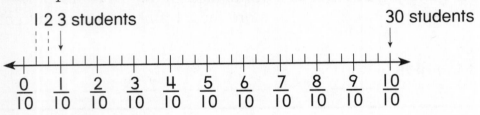

2. Solve the problem.

   Step 1 If $\frac{10}{10} = 30$ students, $\frac{1}{10} = 3$ students who chose playing video games.

   Step 2 If $\frac{1}{10} = 3$ students, $\frac{3}{10} =$ _____ 3×3, or 9 _____ students who
   chose watching television.

   If $\frac{3}{5}$ is equivalent to $\frac{6}{10}$, then $\frac{6}{10} =$ __ 3×6, or 18 __ students who
   chose going on-line.

   Step 3 Subtract to find how many more students chose going on-line to
   watching television. __ $18 - 9 = 9$; more students chose going __
   __ on-line. __

Solve the multistep problems.

3. Jay's Video rents 6 videotapes for
   $19.20. Kim's Video rents 6
   videotapes for $18.48. What is the
   difference in price per videotape
   at the two stores?

   _____ $0.12 per videotape _____

4. The schools in Harrison use
   different on-line services: $\frac{7}{12}$ of the
   schools use OK Online; $\frac{1}{6}$ use USA
   Online, and $\frac{1}{4}$ use Go Online. There
   are 12 schools in Harrison. How
   many schools use each service?

   _____ 7 OK Online; 2 USA Online; _____
   _____ 3 Go Online _____

Estimating Sums and Differences

Write the correct answer.

1. Round the mixed number $3\frac{3}{8}$ to the nearest $\frac{1}{2}$ or whole number.

$$3\frac{1}{2}$$

2. Round the mixed numbers and estimate the sum.

$4\frac{1}{10} + 5\frac{7}{8} = $ _?_

$$10$$

3. Of the students who attend a play, $\frac{3}{8}$ have seen the play already and another $\frac{3}{8}$ have read it. Write a fraction in simplest form for the part of the students who have seen or read the play already.

$$\frac{3}{4}$$

4. The team orders pizza with 16 slices. Two slices have mushrooms, two have olives, six have sausage, and six have broccoli. Write a fraction in simplest form for the part of the pizza that has sausage or mushrooms.

$$\frac{1}{2}$$

Choose the letter of the correct answer.

5. What is the most reasonable estimate of the difference?

$7\frac{2}{9} - 3\frac{5}{8} = $ _?_

A $3\frac{1}{2}$ **B** 5   **C** $4\frac{1}{2}$ **D** $2\frac{1}{2}$

6. What is the most reasonable estimate of the sum?

$8\frac{1}{5} + 6\frac{8}{9} = $ _?_

F 1   **G** $16\frac{1}{2}$ **(H)** 15   **J** 17

7. Five friends play a game. They choose a 2-digit number (10–99) at random. A player scores a point when the number fits into her category. Who is most likely to win?

A Leona: a multiple of 7
B Annette: a factor of 96
C Sally: a number with 3 in it
D Jill: a factor of 64
E Barbara: a number with 0 in it

8. Sid signs on to the Internet at 42 seconds after 2:38 P.M. He signs off at 9 seconds after 2:52 P.M. His Internet service provider rounds the time spent online to the nearest minute. If the charge is $0.04 per minute, how much did Sid's time online cost?

F $0.48   **(G)** $0.52   **H** $0.56
J $0.60   **K** Not Here

9. **Write About It**   Describe the method you used to solve Problem 8.

Possible answer: I counted 18 sec from 2:38:42 to 2:39, 13 min to 2:52,

then I added 9 sec for a total of 13 min, 27 sec, or about 13 min;

$0.04 × 13 = $0.52.

Adding Mixed Numbers

Write the correct answer.

1. Write the sum in simplest form.

   $5\frac{3}{8} + 2\frac{1}{4} = $ ___?___

   $7\frac{5}{8}$

2. Write the sum in simplest form.

   $7\frac{1}{5} + 4\frac{3}{10} = $ ___?___

   $11\frac{1}{2}$

3. Jared's doughnut recipe calls for $2\frac{1}{8}$ cups of flour and $1\frac{3}{8}$ cups of sugar. Estimate the total number of cups of these ingredients the recipe calls for.

   $3\frac{1}{2}$ c

4. Helena buys $8\frac{1}{2}$ yards of fabric. She uses $6\frac{1}{3}$ yards to reupholster a living room chair. Estimate the number of yards of fabric she has left.

   about 2 yd

Choose the letter of the correct answer.

5. What is the sum in simplest form?

   $3\frac{5}{6} + 8\frac{2}{3} = $ ___?___

   A $11\frac{1}{2}$ B $10\frac{9}{6}$

   C $12\frac{5}{6}$ (D) $12\frac{1}{2}$

6. What is the sum in simplest form?

   $\frac{9}{10} + 2\frac{3}{5} = $ ___?___

   (F) $3\frac{1}{2}$ G $2\frac{15}{10}$

   H $3\frac{5}{10}$ J $12\frac{3}{10}$

7. I am a 3-digit number. The sum of my digits is 10. My first digit and my last digit are the same. One of my factors is 7. What number am I?

   A 181
   B 262
   (C) 343
   D 505
   E 676

8. Carly pays $899 for a computer. Sales tax is $0.05 on every dollar. What will Carly's total cost be?

   (F) $943.95
   G $928.75
   H $899.05
   J $972.15
   K Not Here

9. **Write About It** Explain how you knew whether the sum was in simplest form in Problem 1.

   Possible answer: I looked at the numerator and denominator in the sum; in

   Problem 1, there was no number they were both divisible by (other than 1).

Subtracting Mixed Numbers

Write the correct answer.

1. Write the difference in simplest form.

$7\frac{3}{4} - 2\frac{1}{8} =$ ___?___

$5\frac{5}{8}$

2. Write the difference in simplest form.

$4\frac{1}{5} - \frac{1}{10} =$ ___?___

$4\frac{1}{10}$

3. Olivia walks in the Memorial Day parade. She walks $3\frac{3}{4}$ miles along the parade route, then $1\frac{3}{4}$ miles home. How far does she walk in all?

$5\frac{1}{2}$ miles

4. Alan's dog weighs $12\frac{3}{16}$ lb when Alan first gets him. Six months later, he weighs $15\frac{1}{2}$ lb. Estimate the amount of weight gained.

about $3\frac{1}{2}$ lb

Choose the letter of the correct answer.

5. What is the difference in simplest form?

$4\frac{2}{3} - 3\frac{1}{12} =$ ___?___

A $1\frac{2}{3}$ **B** $1\frac{1}{3}$

C $1\frac{7}{12}$ **D** $1\frac{3}{4}$

6. What is the sum in simplest form?

$\frac{9}{12} + 6\frac{1}{6} =$ ___?___

F $15\frac{1}{4}$ **G** $6\frac{11}{12}$

H $7\frac{1}{12}$ **J** $6\frac{5}{6}$

7. Mavis cuts 22 oranges into fourths for the holiday fair. At the end of the fair, 18 of these sections are left, and Mavis eats 6 of them. Which expression could you use to find the number of oranges eaten?

A $22 - (\frac{18}{4} - \frac{6}{4})$ **B** $(22 - \frac{18}{4}) - \frac{6}{4}$

C $(\frac{18}{4} + \frac{6}{4}) + 22$ **D** $22 - (\frac{18}{4} + \frac{6}{4})$

E Not Here

8. Brenda pours $\frac{1}{2}$ of a bottle of soda into a punch bowl. Then she pours two 8-oz cups for Tim and Ellen. She pours 4 oz for her mother, 4 oz for her father, and $\frac{1}{2}$ of what is left for her sister. There is just enough left for Brenda to have a 4-oz cup. How much soda was in the bottle when she started?

F 64 oz   **G** 96 oz   **H** 128 oz

J 32 oz   **K** Not Here

9. **Write About It** Describe the method you used to solve Problem 8.

<u>**Possible answer: I worked backward: I started with Brenda's 4 oz, doubled**</u>

<u>**it, added 4 oz twice, added 8 oz twice, then doubled that for a total of 64 oz.**</u>

Sequencing

Putting events in order, or in **sequence**, can help you
solve a problem. Words like *first, second, next,* and *then*
can help set the order. Read the following problem.

> Soccer practice starts at 3:00. May spent the first part
> of soccer practice stretching. Then she spent $\frac{1}{3}$ hour
> on passing. After that, she spent $\frac{1}{4}$ hour running. Then
> she played a practice game which lasted $\frac{2}{3}$ of an hour.
> She was at practice for $1\frac{3}{4}$ hours. What time did May
> finish stretching?

1. List each activity and its length of time in order. Record a
   question mark where you need to find an answer.

   Event 1: Stretching: ___?___   Event 2: __Passing: $\frac{1}{3}$ hr__

   Event 3: __Running: $\frac{1}{4}$ hr__   Event 4: __Practice game: $\frac{2}{3}$ hr__

   Total practice: $1\frac{3}{4}$ hours

2. How does knowing the order help you figure out how to
   solve the problem? __Possible answer: You need to know the total of the__
   __times for Events 2–4 so you can subtract it from the total practice time__
   __to find the time for Event 1.__

3. Solve the problem. __$\frac{1}{3}$ hr = 20 min; $\frac{1}{4}$ hr = 15 min; $\frac{2}{3}$ hr = 40 min;__
   __20 + 15 + 40 = 75; $1\frac{3}{4}$ hr = 105 min; 105 − 75 = 30 min or $\frac{1}{2}$ hr__
   __stretching. So, she finished stretching at 3:30.__

4. Describe the problem-solving strategy you used. __Possible answer:__
   __I worked backward.__

Sequence the events. Solve. Check students' sequences.

5. Jim told his father to pick any
   number. Then Jim told him to
   multiply it by 3, then add 5, then
   divide by 2, then subtract 4. Jim's
   father said the result was 6. Jim
   told his father the starting number
   he picked. What was the number?

   __The number that Jim's father__

   __picked was 5.__

6. Nona ran in a race from Oil Town
   to Eco-Vill. She ran from Oil Town
   to Queens. She ran $3\frac{1}{2}$ mi from
   Queens to Wayside. She ran 6 mi
   from Wayside to Rigby and $2\frac{1}{2}$ mi
   from Rigby to Eco-Village. The
   race was $15\frac{1}{2}$ mi. How far was it
   from Oil Town to Queens?

   __Oil Town to Queens was $3\frac{1}{2}$ mi.__

Changing Customary Units

Write the correct answer.

1. Change the unit.

   15 ft = __?__ yd

   _____ 5 _____

2. Change the unit.

   3 mi = __?__ yd

   _____ 5,280 _____

3. Dale glues together two pieces of wood to make a tabletop. One measures $1\frac{1}{2}$ inches thick. The other measures $1\frac{3}{4}$ inches thick. How thick will the tabletop be?

   $3\frac{1}{4}$ in. thick

4. Jon has a strip of molding that measures $14\frac{3}{4}$ inches long. He cuts off a $7\frac{3}{8}$-inch length of it. What is the new length of the strip?

   $7\frac{3}{8}$ in.

Choose the letter of the correct answer.

5. Which measurement is equivalent to 15 yards?

   A 45 in.   B 45 yd

   C 45 ft   D 5 ft

6. Which measurement is equivalent to 84 inches?

   F 2 yd   G 12 ft

   H 7 ft   J 3 yd

7. The perimeter of Mr. Werner's square backyard is greater than 300 ft. Which of the following can *not* be true about his backyard?

   A Its area is 10,000 sq ft.
   B Each edge is at least 75 ft.
   C Its area is 5,000 sq ft.
   D One edge of it is 80 ft.
   E Not Here

8. Of the students in Matt's class, $\frac{3}{4}$ have seen the movie *Home Alone*. What fraction of the students in Matt's class has *not* seen the movie?

   F $\frac{3}{8}$ G $\frac{1}{2}$ H $\frac{1}{4}$

   J $\frac{6}{8}$ K $\frac{4}{6}$

9. **Write About It**   Explain how you knew whether to multiply or divide when changing units in Problems 1 and 2.

   Possible answer: If the unit I change to is smaller, I know I need more of

   it, so I multiply; if it is larger, I know I need fewer, so I divide.

Computing Customary Units

Write the correct answer.

1. Rename the measurement.

   70 in. = _?_ ft _?_ in.

   _____**Possible answer: 5 ft 10 in.**_____

2. Rename the measurement.

   6 ft 6 in. = 5 ft _?_ in.

   _____**18 in.**_____

3. Fabric is sold by the yard. Felice buys 9 yards of fabric for curtains. How many feet of fabric is 9 yards?

   _____**27 ft**_____

4. Irene spends $6\frac{1}{2}$ hours in school each day. Of that time, $3\frac{1}{4}$ hours is spent in her homeroom classroom. How many hours of her school day does Irene spend outside of her homeroom classroom?

   $$3\frac{1}{4} \text{ hr}$$

Choose the letter of the correct answer.

5. What is the sum?

   6 ft 4 in.
   + 4 ft 9 in.

   A 10 ft 1 in.   **B** 11 ft 13 in.
   C 11 ft 1 in.   **D** 11 ft 3 in.

6. What is the sum?

   7 yd 1 ft
   − 3 yd 2 ft

   F 11 yd   **G** 4 yd 1 ft
   H 3 yd 2 ft   **J** 3 yd 4 ft

7. Arthur bikes 3.8 miles each way to school 5 days a week. He bikes another 6.4 miles each way to his grandmother's house on Sunday. How many miles does he bike each week?

   A 25.4 mi
   B 51 mi
   C 38.8 mi
   D 50.8 mi
   E 102 mi

8. Travis has three younger brothers: Mike, Vic, and Daniel. He also has a sister, Louise, who is the middle child. Mike and Daniel are the two children who are closest in age. Which of the following could show their ages from oldest to youngest?

   F Travis, Mike, Louise, Daniel, Vic
   G Travis, Vic, Louise, Daniel, Mike
   H Travis, Louise, Mike, Daniel, Vic
   J Louise, Travis, Vic, Mike, Daniel
   K Not Here

9. **Write About It**   Describe the steps you took to solve Problem 6.

   _____**Possible answer: I tried to subtract the feet; 2 > 1, so I had to rename**_____

   _____**7 yd 1 ft as 6 yd 4 ft; then I subtracted the feet (4 ft − 2 ft = 2 ft) and the**_____

   _____**yards (6 yd − 3 yd = 3 yd).**_____

Capacity

Write the correct answer.

1. Change the unit.

16 fl oz = __?__ c

_____ **2 c** _____

2. Change the unit.

5 gal = __?__ pt

_____ **40 pt** _____

3. Carol has a $2\frac{1}{4}$-hour radio show. $1\frac{1}{8}$ hours is devoted to music. The rest is devoted to talk. How many hours of Carol's show are devoted to talk?

_____ $1\frac{1}{8}$ **hr** _____

4. On Tuesday, Jean runs 3 miles 400 yards on the school track. Philippe runs 5 miles 200 yards. How much farther does Philippe run?

_____ **1 mi 1,560 yd** _____

Choose the letter of the correct answer.

5. Which is the greatest measurement of capacity?

A 2 gal   **B** 12 qt
C 26 pt   **D** 44 c

6. Which measurement is equal to 128 fluid ounces?

F 2 qt   **G** 16 pt
H 1 gal   **J** 32 c

7. Ray and Bob are driving 1,200 miles by car. They drive at an average speed of 55 miles per hour. How long will the drive take, to the nearest whole hour?

A 18 hr
B 19 hr
C 20 hr
D 22 hr
E 24 hr

8. Connie's new car gets 32 miles to a gallon of gasoline. About how many fluid ounces of gasoline does the car use to drive 1 mile?

F 4 fl oz
G 6 fl oz
H 8 fl oz
J 2 fl oz
K Not Here

9. Write About It Explain the steps you took to solve Problem 6.

Possible answer: First I renamed 128 fl oz as cups by dividing:

128 ÷ 8 = 16 c; then I compared 16 c to quarts, pints, and gallons:

16 c = 8 pt = 4 qt = 1 gal.

_____

_____

Weight

Write the correct answer.

1. Write *tons*, *pounds*, or *ounces* to describe the weight of a box of crackers.

_____ **ounces** _____

2. Change the unit.

64 oz = __?__ lb

_____ **4 lb** _____

3. Doug buys a six-pack of 12-ounce cans of soda. Dawn buys a half-gallon bottle of soda. Who buys more soda?

_____ **Doug** _____

4. Julie measures the width of her classroom as 290 inches. What is the width of the classroom in feet?

_____ **24 ft 2 in.** _____

Choose the letter of the correct answer.

5. Which measurement is equivalent to 22 pounds?

A 0.1 T   B 488 oz
C 192 oz   (D) 352 oz

6. Which measurement is equivalent to 6 tons?

F 3,000 lb   (G) 12,000 lb
H 32,000 oz   J 6,000 lb

7. Which measurement is equivalent to 64 fluid ounces?

(A) 4 pt   B 4 c
C 8 pt   D 16 pt

8. Which measurement is equivalent to 96 inches?

F 6 ft   (G) 8 ft
H 10 ft   J 12 ft

9. The Fernandez quadruplets are all different heights: 6 ft 2 in., 5 ft 10 in., 5 ft 11 in., and 5 ft, 9 in. What is the average height of the Fernandez quadruplets?

A 6 ft   (B) 5 ft 11 in.
C 5 ft 10 in.   D 5 ft 9 in.
E 6 ft 1 in.

10. The average person spends about 8 hours out of every 24 hours asleep. About how many years has a 75-year-old person slept?

(F) about 25 yr   G about 35 yr
H about 18 yr   J about 20 yr
K Not Here

11. **Write About It**   Describe the steps you took to solve Problem 10.

Possible answer: I saw that 8 hours out of 24 hours equals $\frac{1}{3}$, so I

_____

divided 75 by 3 to find $\frac{1}{3}$ of 75 years.

_____

Name _____

Elapsed Time

Write the correct answer.

1. Write the elapsed time from 2:45 A.M. to 4:05 A.M.

   1 hr 20 min

2. Write the time that is 4 hours 40 minutes later than 3:25 P.M.

   8:05 P.M.

3. Justin weighs $88\frac{1}{2}$ pounds. How many ounces is this?

   1,416 oz

4. In Britain, a person's weight is measured using a unit called a *stone*. One stone equals 14 pounds. How many ounces are there in 1 stone?

   224 oz

Choose the letter of the correct answer.

5. Beth takes a bike ride for 2 hours 45 minutes. She gets home at 11:20 A.M. Which time shows the time she started?

   A 9:05 A.M.
   B 8:40 A.M.
   C 8:35 A.M.
   D 7:35 A.M.

6. Which is the date that is 17 days after the first Thursday of March?

March						
Sun	Mon	Tues	Wed	Thur	Fri	Sat
		1	2	3	4	5
6	7	8	9	10	11	12
13	14	15	16	17	18	19
20	21	22	23	24	25	26
27	28	29	30	31		

   F Tues, Mar 22   G Sun, Mar 20
   H Sat, Mar 19   J Mon, Mar 21

7. Sally has 5 colors of socks mixed up in her drawer. One morning she reaches into the drawer in the dark. How many socks must she take out to be sure she has at least 2 socks of the same color?

   F 2 socks   G 6 socks
   H 7 socks   J 8 socks
   K Not Here

8. Ralph weighs 120 lb. On the moon, Ralph would weigh only $\frac{1}{6}$ his weight, or 20 lb. Neil weighs 108 lb. How much would he weigh on the moon?

   A 18 lb   B 16 lb   C 14 lb
   D 19 lb   E 17 lb

9. **Write About It** Explain the reasoning you used to help you solve Problem 7.

   Possible answer: Sally could pick out 5 socks and still not have a match, but when she picks the next sock, it has to match at least 1 of the socks she already has.

Summarizing

When you write a **summary**, you write a shorter version of
the information. A summary of a problem should include
the main ideas and all of the information you need to
solve it. Writing a summary is a helpful way to make sure
you understand the problem. Read the following problem.

> Mr. Khan's class is holding a short-story contest. Each
> day during the week, 6 students will read their
> stories. Each student will have 7 minutes to read. If
> they begin reading at 1:00 P.M., what is the latest time
> they will finish?

1. Write a summary of the problem. Include the main ideas and
   information that will help you solve the problem.

   Summary: _Possible answer: Six students will read their stories for_
   up to 7 minutes each. They will start at 1:00 P.M. At what time
   will they finish?

2. Solve the problem. _6 × 7 = 42; 42 minutes after 1:00 P.M. is 1:42 P.M.;_
   they will finish at no later than 1:42 P.M.

3. Describe the strategy you used. _Possible answer: I multiplied 6 × 7, 42,_
   and added 42 minutes to 1:00.

Write a summary. Solve. **Possible summaries are given.**

4. The third grade uses the school
   playground from 9:45 until 10:30;
   the fifth grade uses it for the next
   40 minutes; and the first grade uses
   it for the next 45 minutes, until the
   school lunch period. At what time
   does lunch period begin?

   The playground is used until

   10:30 A.M. and then also for the

   next 85 minutes. At what time is

   lunch? _11:55 A.M._

5. The train for Denver leaves
   Boulder at 3:10 P.M. It will take
   Jack 45 minutes to drive from his
   house to the station, 10 minutes to
   park, and 20 minutes to buy a
   ticket and board the train. At what
   time should Jack leave home?

   Jack needs 45 minutes plus

   10 minutes plus 20 minutes to

   make his train that leaves at

   3:10 P.M. When should he leave

   for the train? _1:55 P.M._

Temperature Changes

Write the correct answer.

1. Write the difference in temperature between 72°F and 38°F.

_____ **34°** _____

2. Write the difference in temperature between 69°C and ⁻12°C.

_____ **81°** _____

3. A paint-store clerk tells Troy that a pint of the paint he wants will cover 120 square feet. Troy buys a gallon of the paint. How many square feet should it cover?

_____ **960 sq ft** _____

4. Annette has $19\frac{5}{8}$ inches of silver wire. She cuts an $11\frac{1}{2}$-inch piece for a necklace. How much of the silver wire is left?

_____ $8\frac{1}{8}$ **in.** _____

Choose the letter of the correct answer.

5. The temperature at sunrise is 4°C. The temperature at noon is 28°C. Which choice shows how much the temperature rose from sunrise to noon?

A 22°   (B) 24°
C 26°   D 28°
E. Not Here

6. In Hapsburg, the temperature fell 48°F during a 24-hour period. If the temperature at the start of this period was 39°F, what was the temperature 24 hours later?

(F) ⁻9°F   G ⁻11°F
H 87°F   J 11°F

7. Sabine stands 11 in. from a mirror. The mirror glass is $\frac{1}{4}$ in. thick. How far away does Sabine's reflection appear to be from her?

A 11 in.   B $12\frac{3}{4}$ in.
C 22 in.   D $23\frac{3}{4}$ in.
(E) $22\frac{1}{2}$ in.

8. Sound waves travel about 350 yards per second. Marti sees lightning strike and counts off 10 seconds before she hears the thunder. About how many miles is she away from the lightning strike? (Remember: There are 1,760 yards in 1 mile.)

F about $\frac{1}{2}$ mi   G about 1 mi
(H) about 2 mi   J about 5 mi

9. **Write About It**   Describe the steps you took to solve Problem 6.

<u>Possible answer: To subtract 48 degrees from 39°, I counted down</u>

<u>39° to 0 on a thermometer and then counted below zero until I got to 48°</u>

<u>in all, or ⁻9°</u>

Multiplying Fractions and Whole Numbers

Write the correct answer.

1. Solve.

   $\frac{3}{4} \times 16 = \underline{\ ?\ }$

   _____ 12 _____

2. Solve.

   $40 \times \frac{3}{10} = \underline{\ ?\ }$

   _____ 12 _____

3. Math class starts at 9:50 A.M. and ends at 10:45 A.M. How long is the class?

   _____ 55 min _____

4. Nate's room is 12 feet 3 inches long by 10 feet 9 inches wide. What is the perimeter of the room?

   _____ 46 ft _____

Choose the letter of the correct answer.

5. $24 \times \frac{5}{6} = \underline{\ ?\ }$

   (A) 20   **B** 22   **C** 18   **D** 16

6. $\frac{5}{8} \times 32 = \underline{\ ?\ }$

   F 22   **G** 24   **H** 18   **(J)** 20

7. Jennifer has 15 books. Of these books, $\frac{3}{5}$ are adventure books. How many books are adventure books?

   A 6 books
   (B) 9 books
   C 12 books
   D 15 books
   E Not Here

8. Dale's garden has a perimeter of 30 feet. Which of the following can *not* be true about her garden?

   F Its area is 54 sq ft.
   G One side is 9 ft.
   H Each side is less than 30 ft.
   (J) Its area is 100 sq ft.

9. A land developer has a 16-acre plot. She will sell it in 48 equal-size lots for houses. How many acres will each lot be?

   A $\frac{1}{4}$ acre   **B** 1 acre

   (C) $\frac{1}{3}$ acre   **D** $\frac{2}{3}$ acre

   E $\frac{1}{8}$ acre

10. In one week, Evan works 40 hours at $6.50 per hour. He also works 6 hours overtime. Overtime pay is 1.5 times Evan's pay rate. How much does Evan earn during the week?

    F $310.00   **(G)** $318.50
    H $385.00   **J** $358.50
    K Not Here

11. **Write About It**   Explain how you multiplied a whole number by a fraction in Problem 5.

    Possible answer: I first found $\frac{1}{6}$ of 24 by dividing: 24 ÷ 6 = 4; I then

    multiplied this quotient by 5 to get $\frac{5}{6}$: 4 × 5 = 20, so $\frac{5}{6}$ of 24 = 20.

More About Multiplying a Fraction by a Fraction

Write the correct answer.

1. Solve. You may shade the fraction squares to help you.

$\frac{2}{3} \times \frac{3}{4} = $ _?_

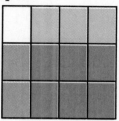

$\frac{6}{12}$, or $\frac{1}{2}$

2. Solve. You may shade the fraction squares to help you.

$\frac{3}{5} \times \frac{3}{5} = $ _?_

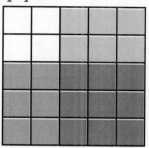

$\frac{9}{25}$

3. Janice stacks twelve $\frac{3}{4}$-inch thick boards. How high is the stack?

9 in.

4. In Detroit the temperature is ⁻12°F. In New Orleans, the temperature is 82°F. What is the difference in the two temperatures?

94°

Choose the letter of the correct answer.

5. What is the product in simplest form?

$\frac{7}{16} \times \frac{1}{4} = $ _?_

A $\frac{7}{4}$ **B** $\frac{7}{64}$ C $\frac{4}{7}$ D $1\frac{3}{4}$

6. What is the product in simplest form?

$\frac{4}{9} \times \frac{3}{8} = $ _?_

F $1\frac{1}{36}$ G $\frac{12}{72}$ **H** $\frac{1}{6}$ J $\frac{3}{8}$

7. Nina has a block of wood that is $\frac{3}{4}$ foot long. Nina will use $\frac{1}{3}$ of it to make boxes. How much of the block will she use?

A $\frac{1}{3}$ ft   B $\frac{1}{8}$ ft   C $\frac{4}{7}$ ft

D $\frac{1}{4}$ ft   E $\frac{3}{4}$ ft

8. Lauren publishes a 7-page magazine article. Each page has 850 words on it. How many words does the article contain in all?

F 5,959   G 6,000
H 8,500   J 59,500
K Not Here

9. **Write About It** Explain how to use the fraction model to solve Problem 1.

Possible answer: The grid has 3 rows, so shade 2 to represent $\frac{2}{3}$; it

has 4 columns, so shade 3 to represent $\frac{3}{4}$. The part shaded twice is

the product, $\frac{6}{12}$, or $\frac{1}{2}$.

Multiplying Fractions and Mixed Numbers

Write the correct answer.

1. Solve. You may shade the fraction squares to help you.

$$\frac{1}{3} \times 1\frac{2}{5} = \underline{\ ?\ }$$

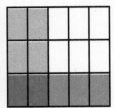

$$\frac{7}{15}$$

2. Solve. You may shade the fraction squares to help you.

$$\frac{3}{4} \times 1\frac{2}{3} = \underline{\ ?\ }$$

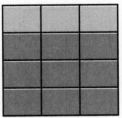

$$\frac{15}{12}, \text{ or } 1\frac{3}{12}, \text{ or } 1\frac{1}{4}$$

3. Lucy has a 1-yard square of carpet. She cuts out a piece that is $\frac{2}{3}$ yard by $\frac{1}{4}$ yard. What is the area of the piece she cuts out?

$$\frac{1}{6} \text{ sq yd}$$

4. A mile equals 5,280 feet. How many square feet are there in 1 square mile?

27,878,400 sq ft

Choose the letter of the correct answer.

5. What is the product in simplest form?

$$\frac{2}{5} \times 1\frac{3}{4} = \underline{\ ?\ }$$

A $\frac{7}{10}$ **B** $\frac{14}{20}$ **C** $1\frac{1}{5}$ **D** $1\frac{3}{7}$

6. What is the product in simplest form?

$$\frac{1}{2} \times 2\frac{3}{8} = \underline{\ ?\ }$$

F $1\frac{3}{8}$ **G** $2\frac{3}{16}$ **H** $\frac{11}{8}$ **J** $1\frac{3}{16}$

7. Joe has tiles that are $\frac{3}{4}$ inch by $3\frac{1}{2}$ inches. What is the area of each tile?

A $2\frac{5}{8}$ sq in. **B** $6\frac{1}{2}$ sq in.

C $3\frac{1}{2}$ sq in. **D** $2\frac{1}{4}$ sq in.

E $9\frac{3}{4}$ sq in.

8. Tim puts fence posts at 1-yard intervals around an 18-foot by 24-foot enclosure. How many posts does he use?

F 28 posts **G** 24 posts
H 18 posts **J** 12 posts
K Not Here

9. **Write About It** What strategy did you use to solve Problem 8?

Possible answer: First I renamed the measures by using yards: 6 yd by 8 yd. I then drew a 6-by-8 rectangle on grid paper and counted the 28 post locations.

Harcourt Brace School Publishers

Making Generalizations

When you **generalize**, you make a statement that is true about a whole group of similar situations. Making a generalization about a problem may give you a clue about the problem's solution. Read the following problem.

VOCABULARY
generalize

Carla needs $9\frac{1}{2}$ m of canvas to make a tent. She will make another tent that is $\frac{2}{3}$ as big. How many meters of canvas will she need to make the smaller tent?

1. Circle the statement that is a generalization for this problem and for similar problems.

   Generalization: Carla will make two tents. She needs $9\frac{1}{2}$ m plus two thirds of $9\frac{1}{2}$ m for both.

   Generalization: The smaller item is a fractional part of the larger item. When I multiply the size of the larger item by the fraction, I will find the size of the smaller item.

   Generalization: The least common denominator of $\frac{1}{2}$ and $\frac{1}{3}$ is sixths.

2. Solve the problem. $\frac{2}{3}$ of $9\frac{1}{2} = \frac{2}{3} \times \frac{19}{2} = \frac{38}{6} = 6\frac{2}{6} = 6\frac{1}{3}$ m of canvas

3. Describe the strategy you used. **Possible answer: I made a model of the fractions.**

Make a generalization about the problem. Solve.

4. Mario's canoe measures 12 feet long. It is $\frac{1}{6}$ as wide as it is long. How wide is Mario's canoe?

   The smaller measurement is a

   fractional part of the larger

   measurement; multiplying;

   2 ft wide.

5. Serge has 24 yards of cloth. He wants to use $\frac{3}{4}$ of the cloth for a banner. How many feet of cloth will he have left after he makes the banner?

   The smaller measurement is a

   fractional part of the larger

   measurement; multiplying;

   18 ft.

Line Relationships

Write the correct answer.

1. Name the point where line AB and line segment ZY intersect.

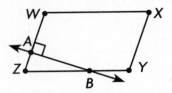

_____
point **B**

2. Name two pairs of intersecting lines.

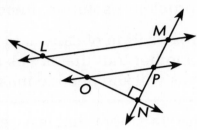

_____
Possible answer:
_____
$\overleftrightarrow{LN}$ and $\overleftrightarrow{OP}$; $\overleftrightarrow{LM}$ and $\overleftrightarrow{MN}$

3. In the figure in Problem 1, name two perpendicular line segments.

Possible answer: $\overline{AB}$ and $\overline{WZ}$

4. Write *parallel* or *perpendicular* to describe lines LN and NM in the figure in Problem 2.

perpendicular

Choose the letter of the correct answer.

5. Look at the figure in Problem 1. Which line segment is parallel to line segment WZ?

A $\overline{WX}$ B $\overline{AB}$ (C)$\overline{XY}$ D $\overline{ZY}$

6. Look at the figure in Problem 2. Which word best describes the relationship of lines LM and OP?

F perpendicular
G intersecting
(H)parallel
J none of the above

7. Draw a rectangle. Label it $ABCD$. Which of the following can you see in your rectangle?

A perpendicular line segments
B intersecting line segments
C parallel line segments
D points
(E)all of the above

8. Shelly's salary is $27,000 a year. How much does she earn per month?

(F)$2,250.00   G $225.00
H $1,200.00   J $2,000.00

9. **Write About It** Which of the lines in the diagram in Problem 1 lie in the same plane? Explain.

Possible answer: All of them. The plane is represented by the sheet of

paper.

Rays and Angles

Write the correct answer.

1. Write the names of the rays in the figure below.

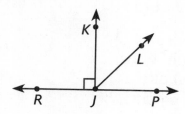

   $\overrightarrow{JP}$, $\overrightarrow{JL}$, $\overrightarrow{JK}$, and $\overrightarrow{JR}$

2. Write the names of three parallel lines in the figure below.

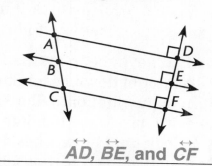

   $\overleftrightarrow{AD}$, $\overleftrightarrow{BE}$, and $\overleftrightarrow{CF}$

3. Write the names of the acute angles in the figure in Problem 1.

   $\angle KJL$ and $\angle LJP$

4. Write the names of a pair of perpendicular lines in the figure in Problem 2.

   Possible answer: $\overleftrightarrow{CF}$ and $\overleftrightarrow{FD}$

Choose the letter of the correct answer.

5. Which angle in the figure in Problem 1 is an obtuse angle?

   A $\angle RJK$ B $\angle KJP$
   C $\angle LJP$ (D) $\angle RJL$

6. Which angle in the figure in Problem 2 is a right angle?

   F $\angle ACF$ (G) $\angle FDA$
   H $\angle DAC$ J $\angle EBA$

7. Think about the kinds of angles the hands on a clock form at different times during the day. At which of these times do the hands form an obtuse angle?

   A 6:00   B 6:16   C 6:32
   (D) 6:08   E 12:00

8. Imagine that the next time you hear someone say the word "clock," you look at a clock. Which word best describes the chance that at that moment, the clock's hands will be forming a right angle?

   (F) unlikely   G likely
   H certain   J impossible
   K Not Here

9. **Write About It** What strategy did you use to solve Problem 7?

   Possible answer: I acted out the different times with the hands of a clock to see what angles the given times formed.

Interpreting Symbols

Symbols are signs that are used instead of words. A problem might include symbols such as = for *equal to*, or < for *less than*. Sometimes you will need to find out what a symbol means. You can look it up in the glossary at the back of your book. Read the following problem.

Aaron had never been to Chad's house. Chad told him to walk straight down Main Street for 4 blocks, make a 90° turn to the right onto Elm Street and walk 2 blocks, make a 90° turn to the left onto Acorn Street, and then walk $\frac{1}{2}$ block until he reaches 54 Acorn Street. Aaron made a map of the directions. Draw the map. **Check students' maps.**

1. Find a symbol in the problem above.

   Draw the symbol you found. __°__

   Tell what the symbol means. __degree__

   How does knowing the meaning of the symbol help you draw a map or a diagram? **Possible answer: 90° is a right angle. When I make the map, I will make a right angle when called for.**

2. Solve the problem. __Check students' maps.__

3. Describe the strategy you used. __I drew a map or diagram.__

Circle the symbol in each problem and tell what it means. Then solve.

4. From Turtle Island, the captain went north, steering the boat 40° east. He traveled 2 km and then steered the boat 15° north. He traveled 6 km and steered the boat 10° west. Make a map of the boat's course.

   __degrees; check students' maps.__

5. Sam said he could draw an equilateral triangle and label each line segment $\overline{AB}$, $\overline{BC}$, $\overline{CA}$. Are the line segments congruent? Make Sam's drawing and explain.

   __line segment; yes; check student's drawings; because an equilateral triangle has all sides of equal length.__

Name _____

Classifying Quadrilaterals

Write the correct answer.

1. Name the quadrilateral that has two pairs of congruent sides and four right angles.

_____ **rectangle** _____

2. Name the quadrilateral that has exactly one pair of parallel sides.

_____ **trapezoid** _____

3. How many acute angles are there in a parallelogram that is not a rectangle?

_____ **2 acute angles** _____

4. How many pairs of perpendicular lines are there in a square?

_____ **4 pairs** _____

Choose the letter of the correct answer.

5. Which quadrilateral is a parallelogram with right angles and congruent sides?

(A) a square
B a rectangle
C a trapezoid
D a rhombus

6. Which of the following *cannot* be a parallelogram?

F a square
G a rectangle
H a rhombus
(J) a trapezoid

7. Suppose you know that at least two of a quadrilateral's angles are right angles. Which of the following can you conclude?

A It is a rectangle.
B It is a square.
C It is a parallelogram.
D It is not a trapezoid.
(E) None of the Above

8. Let d stand for a number of dogs. Suppose e is the number of ears, t is the number of tails, and p is the number of paws. Which choice shows the relationships among these letters?

F $e = d; t = 2 \times d; p = 4 \times d$
G $e = 2 \times d; t = d; p = 2 \times d$
(H) $e = 2 \times d; t = d; p = 4 \times d$
J $e = 4 \times d; t = 2 \times d; p = 8 \times d$
K Not Here

9. **Write About It** Suppose d in Problem 8 equals 6. Write the values of the other three letters.

$e = 12; t = 6; p = 24$

Name _____

Classifying Triangles

Write the correct answer.

1. Name the triangle. Write *isosceles*, *scalene*, or *equilateral*.

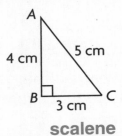

_____scalene_____

2. Name the triangle. Write *isosceles*, *scalene*, or *equilateral*.

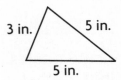

_____isosceles_____

3. Write the names of the two sides that are perpendicular in triangle *ABC* in Problem 1.

_____*AB* and *BC*_____

4. Write *acute*, *right*, or *obtuse* to describe the angles in the triangle in Problem 2.

_____acute_____

Choose the letter of the correct answer.

5. What word describes a triangle that has exactly two sides congruent?

A scalene   **(B)** isosceles
C right   **D** obtuse

6. What word describes an angle whose measure is greater than a right angle?

F acute   **(G)** obtuse
H scalene   **J** right

7. Two angles of a parallelogram are acute. What can you conclude about the parallelogram's other two angles?

A They are right angles.
B They are also acute.
(C) They are obtuse.
D One of them may be a right angle.
E Not Here

8. Tonya's salary is $3,200 a month. From each paycheck, $894 is taken out for taxes, $233 for Social Security, and $185 for insurance. How much of her paycheck is left over?

(F) $1,888
G $1,978
H $2,318
J $1,658
K Not Here

9. Write About It Explain the strategy you used to solve Problem 7.

Possible answer: I drew pictures of parallelograms with two acute angles,

trying to see what had to be true about the other two angles.

More About Classifying Triangles

Write the correct answer.

1. Write *right*, *acute*, or *obtuse* to describe the triangle.

_____ right _____

2. Write *right*, *acute*, or *obtuse* to describe the triangle.

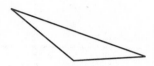

_____ obtuse _____

3. Write *intersecting*, *parallel*, or *perpendicular*, to describe the relationship that rungs on a ladder have to each other.

_____ parallel _____

4. Jennifer says that her yard is a parallelogram *and* a rectangle *and* a rhombus. Must her yard also be a square?

_____ yes _____

Choose the letter of the correct answer.

5. A triangle has one angle that measures 85° and another that measures 35°. What is the measure of the triangle's third angle?

   A 25°   B 50°   C 150°   (D) 60°

6. A painter climbs a ladder that is leaning against a building. Which type of triangle does the ladder form with the building and the ground?

   (F) right   G acute
   H obtuse   J equilateral

7. Which triangle is it impossible to draw?

   A isosceles right triangle
   B scalene right triangle
   (C) obtuse right triangle
   D scalene obtuse triangle
   E isosceles obtuse triangle

8. A bicyclist rides 700 miles in 5 days. She bikes the same distance each day. If she bikes for 7 hours a day, what is her average speed?

   F 10 mph   G 15 mph
   H 25 mph   (J) 20 mph
   K Not Here

9. **Write About It**   Explain why it is impossible to draw the triangle you chose as your answer to Problem 7.

Possible answer: If a triangle has a right angle, the measures of the other two angles must add up to 90°; for the triangle to be obtuse, one of those angles would have to be greater than 90°.

Testing for Congruence

Write the correct answer.

1. Write *congruent* or *not congruent* to describe the figures.

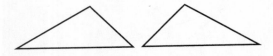

__congruent__

2. Write *congruent* or *not congruent* to describe the figures.

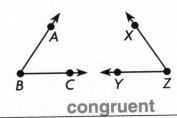

__congruent__

3. Write *equilateral, isosceles,* or *scalene* to describe the triangles in Problem 1.

__scalene__

4. Write *acute, right,* or *obtuse* to describe ∠ABC in Problem 2.

__acute__

Choose the letter of the correct answer.

5. A triangle has one 45° angle and one 65° angle. Which is the measure of the triangle's third angle?

A 80°   **B** 70°   C 60°   D 40°

6. Which word best describes the triangles in Problem 1?

F acute   G right
H obtuse   J isosceles

7. Nick and Doreen ordered a square pizza. Nick cut it into 6 equal rows. Then he made 4 equal cuts perpendicular to the rows. He ate 6 pieces and Doreen ate 4. Which fraction shows the part of the pizza they ate?

A $\frac{5}{6}$ B $\frac{10}{12}$ **C** $\frac{1}{3}$

D $\frac{3}{8}$ E $\frac{5}{6}$

8. Which figures are *not* always congruent?

F the opposite sides of a rectangle
G right angles
H all angles in an equilateral triangle
J all sides in an equilateral triangle
K Not Here

9. **Write About It**   Explain how you solved Problem 5.

__Possible answer: I know that the sum of the measures of the three angles__

__in a triangle is 180°, so I subtracted: 180 − 45 = 135; 135 − 65 = 70.__

__The angle is 70°.__

Congruence and Symmetry

Write the correct answer.

1. Write how many lines of symmetry the figure has.

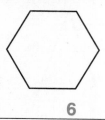

_____ 6 _____

2. Write how many lines of symmetry the figure has.

_____ 1 _____

3. How many congruent sides does the figure in Problem 1 have?

_____ 6 _____

4. The logo for a company is a parallelogram that has 4 congruent sides but no right angles. What is another name for this figure?

_____ **a rhombus** _____

Choose the letter of the correct answer.

5. What tool is used to measure angles?

A compass   **B** ruler
C square   **D** protractor

6. A right triangle has an angle that measures 52°. What is the measure of the triangle's third angle?

F 48°   **G** 38°   **H** 28°   **J** 58°

7. A senior-citizen choral group has 7 members. The members' ages are 72, 65, 77, 72, 86, 78, and 82. What is the average age of the members?

A 74   **B** 73   **C** 79
D 75   **E** 76

8. Which letter has both point symmetry and line symmetry?

F F   **G** G
H O   **J** J
K Not Here

9. Write About It Describe how you determine whether a figure has a line of symmetry.

__Possible answer: I see if I can draw a line through it and fold it over on__

__itself so that the halves have matching edges. If so, the figure has a line__

__of symmetry.__

Tessellations

Write the correct answer.

1. Write *tessellates* or *does not tessellate* to describe the figure.

_____tessellates_____

2. Write *tessellates* or *does not tessellate* to describe the figure.

_____tessellates_____

3. How many pairs of parallel line segments are there in the figure in Problem 1?

_____2 pairs_____

4. Write *scalene*, *isosceles*, or *equilateral* to describe the triangle in Problem 2.

_____isosceles_____

Choose the letter of the correct answer.

5. How many lines of symmetry could you draw in the figure in Problem 1?

(A) 0   B 1   C 2   D 4

6. How many lines of symmetry could you draw in the figure in Problem 2?

F 0   (G) 1   H 2   J 4

7. Susan prices cheese at 5 stores. Which store has the best buy on cheese?

A Gourmet Kitchen: 5 oz for $7.95
B Rothschild's: 1 oz for $1.50
C Bragdorf's: 3 oz for $1.99
(D) Food Mart: 8 oz for $11.60
E The Grapevine: 2 oz for $3.10

8. Which of these structures in nature best demonstrates a tessellation pattern?

F a spider web
G a snowflake
H a leopard's spots
(J) a honeycomb
K Not Here

9. Write About It Describe the method you used to solve Problem 7.

Possible answer: I found the price per oz at each store by dividing the

cost by the number of oz; then I compared these to see which was

the least expensive.

Observing Patterns

When you look at a design, see whether the elements of the design form a pattern. **Patterns** are details that repeat in the same order over and over again. Patterns can involve colors, shapes, or numbers. Finding a pattern is often the key to solving a problem. Read the following problem.

VOCABULARY
patterns

Marco made a design using 1 yellow hexagon and 2 green triangles for his pattern. If he uses 3 yellow hexagons in the top row, how many green triangles will he use to complete the row? Make a model to solve.

1. Make a drawing of Marco's design. <u>**Check students' drawings.**</u>

Possible drawing:

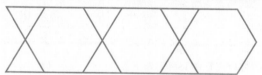

Describe the pattern. <u>**green triangles on two sides of the yellow hexagon**</u>
<u>**make the base unit of the pattern**</u>

2. Solve. <u>**6 green triangles**</u>

3. Describe the strategy you used. <u>**I made a model of the design with**</u>
<u>**pattern blocks.**</u>

Use patterns to solve.

4. Greg drew a quilt design that is shaped like a hexagon. He used 4 different polygons. Use pattern blocks to make a design that Greg could have made. Draw the design.
Check students' drawings.
Possible design:

 hexagon
trapezoid
rhombus
triangle

5. Erin will plant a border around her rectangular yard. The border will have 16 apple trees, with 2 shrubs between trees. Draw a model of the border. How many shrubs will Erin need?

Check students' drawings;
32 shrubs

Name _____

Construct a Circle

Write the correct answer.

1. Write *chord*, *diameter*, or *radius* to describe line segment *AB* in the circle.

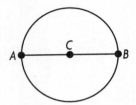

_____diameter (also chord)_____

2. Write *chord*, *diameter*, or *radius* to describe line segment *CB* in the circle.

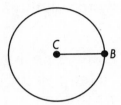

_____radius_____

3. A figure has two right angles. Are the angles congruent?

_____yes_____

4. Is it possible to draw a triangle that has only one acute angle?

_____no_____

Choose the letter of the correct answer.

5. What is the name of a chord that passes through a circle's center?

  A radius   (B) diameter
  C center   D circumference

6. The Venn diagram shows the relationships of some kinds of lines. Which words could replace the letters A, B, and C?

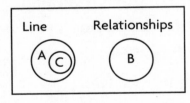

7. Which number comes next in the pattern?

  5, 10, 20, 35, 55, 80, 110, _?_

  A 130
  B 150
  C 140
  D 155
  (E) 145

8. Two angles in a triangle measure 38° and 93°. Which is the measure of the third angle?

  (F) 49°   G 68°   H 119°   J 89°
  K Not Here

  F A, parallel; B, perpendicular; C, intersecting
  G A, perpendicular; B, parallel; C, intersecting
  (H) A, intersecting; B, parallel; C, perpendicular
  J A, intersecting; B, perpendicular; C, parallel

9. **Write About It** Write the rule for the pattern you saw in Problem 7.

  <u>Possible answer: The difference between each pair of numbers is the next</u>

  <u>greatest multiple of 5: 5, 10, 15, 20, 25, and so on; the next term is 110 + 35.</u>

Making Predictions

An **estimate** is an approximate answer to a problem. If a
question asks you to find *about* how many, you can use
estimation to make a prediction. When a problem asks for
an exact answer, you can estimate to check the
reasonableness of your answer. When there are several
ways to solve a problem, estimate to find out if you get
the same answer each way. Read the following problem.

VOCABULARY
estimate

> The students in Kyle's class are decorating cans for the
> windowsills. They will cut sheets of paper to the exact
> size of each can. How can Kyle find out the size of the
> sheet he needs to wrap around a can that is 15
> centimeters in height with a diameter of 8 centimeters?

1. What prediction can you make? **You can estimate the**
   circumference of the can, so you can predict the size of
   the paper needed.

   To find the circumference of the can, multiply the diameter
   by 3.14 (π). What is your estimate for the circumference of
   Kyle's can? **Multiply 8 cm by 3 ; 24 cm.**

   About what size sheet does Kyle need to cover the can?
   about 15 cm by 24 cm

2. Solve. **3.14 $\times$ 8 cm = 25.12 cm; the paper needs to be**
   15 cm high and 25.12 cm long.

3. How did you check your answer? **I found the circumference**
   by using a formula and estimated to check whether my
   answer was reasonable.

Use estimation to make predictions. Solve.

4. Kristin covers a cylinder in blue
   fabric. The cylinder is 11 in. in
   height and its diameter is 6 in.
   About what size should she cut the
   fabric to cover the cylinder?

   about 11 in. by 18 in.

5. Rasheed makes a walkie-talkie
   out of 2 tin cans. Each can has a
   height of 8 inches and a diameter
   of 4 inches. If he covers each tin
   can with paper, how much paper
   will he use?

   two sheets of paper measuring
   8 in. by 12.56 in.

Name _____

Angles in a Circle

Write the correct answer.

1. Two diameters in a circle are perpendicular. What are the measures of the four angles they form?

    Each measures 90°.

2. Two radii in a circle are perpendicular. What are the measures of the two angles they form?

    90° and 270°

3. I am a parallelogram with all congruent sides. One of my angles measures 75°. What figure am I?

    a rhombus

4. Which part of a circle do the hands on a clock suggest at 6:00?

    a diameter

Choose the letter of the correct answer.

5. Three radii in a circle form three angles. Two of the angles measure 40° and 80°. What is the measure of the third angle?

    A 220°   B 300°
    C 160°   D 240°

6. Four radii in a circle form four angles. One of the angles measures 90°. Which can *not* be the measure of any of the three other angles?

    F 280°   G 180°
    H 20°   J 240°

7. Douglas leaves work for lunch at 12:15 P.M. As he leaves, he points to the clock and tells his boss, "I'll be back in 120°." At which time should Douglas's boss expect him back?

    A 1:00 P.M.
    B 12:45 P.M.
    C 12:40 P.M.
    D 12:35 P.M.
    E 12:30 P.M.

8. Fabian's taxes for the year work out to be exactly 0.2 of his total income. If his total income is $36,000, how much are his taxes?

    F $3,600
    G $720
    H $7,200
    J $1,080
    K Not Here

9. **Write About It**   Explain how you solved Problem 7.

    Possible answer: It takes 60 min for the minute hand to complete a circle on a clock. 120° is $\frac{1}{3}$ of the circle; so, $\frac{1}{3}$ of 60 min is 20 min; 20 min after 12:15 P.M. is 12:35 P.M.

Measuring Angles in a Circle

Write the correct answer.

1. Use a protractor to measure the angles in the circle. Write the degree measure of the shaded angle.

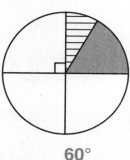

_____ **60°**

2. Use a protractor to draw a second radius in the circle to form a 140° angle. **One possible radii shown.**

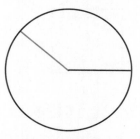

_____ **Check students' drawings.**

3. One of the angles in a right triangle measures 50°. What are the measures of the triangle's other angles?

_____ **40° and 90°** _____

4. What is the measure of each angle in an equilateral triangle?

_____ **60°** _____

Choose the letter of the correct answer.

5. What is the measure of the striped angle in the circle in Problem 1?

A 20° **B** 25° **Ⓒ** 30° **D** 45°

7. During a rainstorm it rains for 45 minutes at the rate of 4 inches per hour. How much did it rain during the 45-minute period?

A 45 in. **B** 4 in.
Ⓒ 3 in. **D** 2 in.
E Not Here

6. What is the sum of the measures of the shaded and striped angles in the circle in Problem 1?

F 60° **G** 120° **Ⓗ** 90° **J** 180°

8. Two brothers shared a pizza. They cut the pizza into 12 slices. Bob ate 4 slices, and Mike ate 5 slices. What fraction of the whole pizza is left?

F $\frac{4}{12}$ **G** $\frac{3}{4}$

H $\frac{2}{3}$ **Ⓙ** $\frac{1}{4}$

9. **Write About It** Explain how you solved Problem 7.

Possible answer: The rainfall rate is given as 4 in. per hr; rain fell for

less than 1 hr, so the total will be less than 4 in. Since 45 min is $\frac{3}{4}$ hr,

I found $\frac{3}{4}$ of the amount of rain that would fall in 1 hr: $\frac{3}{4}$ of 4 = 3.

Prisms and Pyramids

Write the correct answer.

1. Write *prism* or *pyramid* and the name of the polygon that describes the figure's base.

_____ prism; triangle _____

2. Write the name of the solid figure.

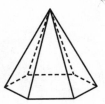

_____ hexagonal pyramid _____

3. You draw 2 radii in a circle that form a 180° angle. What part of the circle have you drawn?

_____ a diameter _____

4. Write *true* or *false:* An obtuse triangle can have a right angle.

_____ false _____

Choose the letter of the correct answer.

5. Which solid figure has a triangular base and 3 triangular faces?

   A triangular prism
   B square pyramid
   C triangular pyramid
   D rectangular prism

6. Which solid figure has 8 faces and 2 bases?

   F hexagonal prism
   G pentagonal pyramid
   H octagonal pyramid
   J octagonal prism

7. Of the 90 students who tried out for the basketball team, only 15 made the final cut. Which fraction shows the part of those who made the final cut?

   A $\frac{5}{9}$ B $\frac{3}{9}$ C $\frac{3}{10}$

   D $\frac{1}{6}$ E $\frac{1}{5}$

8. When Lee gets his paycheck, he pays his $550 rent, his $245 car payment, and his $160 student-loan payment. He deposits $\frac{1}{3}$ of the rest in the bank. He has $320 left. How much is Lee's paycheck?

   F $1,435   G $1,655   H $3,280
   J $1,095   K Not Here

9. **Write About It** Describe the steps you took to solve Problem 7.

   Possible answer: I wrote $\frac{15}{90}$ and looked for the greatest common factor of

   the two numbers to write an equivalent fraction. The GCF is 15, so I divided:

   15 ÷ 15 = 1 and 90 ÷ 15 = 6.

Name _____

Nets for Solid Figures

Write the correct answer.

1. Write the name of the solid figure that the net can be folded to make.

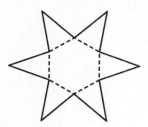

_____hexagonal pyramid_____

2. Write the name of the solid figure that the net can be folded to make.

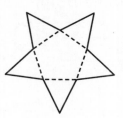

_____pentagonal pyramid_____

3. Write the name of the solid figure that has four congruent triangles.

_____triangular pyramid_____

4. Write the measures of the angles formed by the hands on a clock at 9:00 P.M.

_____90° and 270°_____

Choose the letter of the correct answer.

5. What is the sum of the measures of the four angles created by two perpendicular lines?

A 90°   B 180°
C 270°   (D) 360°

6. Which of these figures will *not* form a tessellation pattern with no gaps?

F square   G rectangle
H triangle   (J) pentagon

7. Toni has a net for a solid figure. It has a triangle in the center and a triangle of the same size off each side of the central triangle. Which solid figure could the net be folded to make?

A hexagonal prism
B triangular prism
C hexagonal pyramid
(D) triangular pyramid
E square pyramid

8. Vince has a net for a rectangular prism. The net has rectangles of three different sizes. They measure 3 cm by 6 cm, 6 cm by 8 cm, and 8 cm by 3 cm. What is the area of the largest face?

F 24 sq cm
G 28 sq cm
H 14 sq cm
(J) 48 sq cm
K Not Here

9. **Write About It** How did you find your answer to Problem 8?

Possible answer: I compared the areas, and the 6-cm by 8-cm face had the greatest area, 48 sq cm.

Algebraic Thinking: Volume

Write the correct answer.

1. The volume of the prism is 96 cubic centimeters. Write the missing dimension.

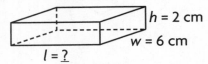

$h = 2$ cm
$w = 6$ cm
$l = \underline{?}$

_____ **8 cm** _____

2. The volume of the prism is 108 cubic meters. Write the missing dimension.

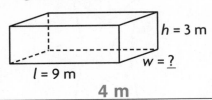

$h = 3$ m
$l = 9$ m
$w = \underline{?}$

_____ **4 m** _____

3. The great pyramids of Egypt are square pyramids. Write the shapes and numbers of their faces and base.

__**1 square base; 4 triangular faces**__

4. A surveyor maps out a triangular plot of land. The plot has angles of 54° and 38°. What is the measure of the plot's third angle?

_____ **88°** _____

Choose the letter of the correct answer.

5. A storage unit measures 8 feet wide by 10 feet deep. The volume of the unit is 720 cubic feet. What is the height of the unit?

   A 90 ft   (B) 9 ft
   C 12 ft   D 10 ft

6. Three radii in a circle form three angles. Two of the angles measure 130° each. What is the measure of the third angle?

   F 240°   G 140°
   H 110°   (J) 100°

7. How many degrees does the minute hand on a clock travel when it moves through one minute?

   (A) 6°   B 9°   C 12°
   D 1°   E 3°

8. Frank gets these scores in six games of golf: 93, 92, 88, 94, 99, and 86. What is his mean score?

   F 89   G 91   (H) 92
   J 90   K Not Here

9. **Write About It** Explain how you solved Problem 7.

   __Possible answer: I know there are 360° in a circle and that there are__

   __60 min in one trip around the clock for the minute hand, so I divided:__

   __360° ÷ 60 = 6°.__

Analyzing Details

When you **analyze** details in a problem, look for
information that is needed to solve the problem.
Underline the important details. Then think about what
clues the details give about how you can solve the
problem. Read the following problem.

VOCABULARY
analyze

> Ms. Ray decides to organize a room in her attic. She
> finds that the room can hold <u>800 cubic feet.</u> If she
> packs various objects in boxes that are each <u>4 feet
> long, 2.5 feet tall</u>, and <u>2 feet wide</u>, how many boxes
> can she put in the room?

1. In the problem above, underline the details that you need to
   solve it.

   What clues do the details give about how to solve the
   problem? **Possible answer: The detail 800 cu ft means that the problem**
   has to do with volume. The dimensions of the boxes are needed to
   find the volume of the boxes.

   _____

   What information do you need to find? **the volume of each box**

   _____

2. Solve. **$V = l \times w \times h$, so $4 \times 2.5 \times 2 = 20$; $800 \div 20 = 40$; 40 boxes**

   _____

3. Describe the strategy you used. **I used the formula for volume,**
   and then I divided.

Underline the details you need to solve each problem. Then solve.

4. Ms. Ray finds an old trunk. She
   wants to pack a stack of photo
   albums. The stack measures
   <u>16 inches long, 12 inches wide,</u>
   <u>and 18 inches high.</u> The trunk
   <u>measures 13 inches wide,</u>
   <u>20 inches high, and 17 inches</u>
   <u>long.</u> Will the albums fit in the
   trunk?

   _____ **yes** _____

5. Ms. Ray puts down shelf paper
   that fits each of <u>5 shelves</u> exactly.
   Each shelf in the closet measures
   <u>4 ft long and $2\frac{1}{2}$ ft wide.</u> How many
   square feet of shelf paper will she
   use?

   _____ **50 sq ft** _____

Name _____

Estimating Volume

Write the correct answer.

1. Which is the most reasonable estimate for the volume of a cereal box—240 cu in., 240 cu ft, or 240 cu yd?

   240 cu in.

2. Which is the most reasonable estimate for the volume of an Olympic-size swimming pool—330 cu in., 330 cu ft, or 330 cu yd?

   330 cu yd

3. A chest is 18 in. wide by 30 in. long. The label on it says its volume is 8,100 cu in. What is the height of the chest?

   15 in.

4. An isosceles triangle has two angles that each measure 35°. What is the measure of the triangle's third angle?

   110°

Choose the letter of the correct answer.

5. A triangle has sides that measure 5 inches, 2 inches, and 5 inches Which name best describes the triangle?

   A scalene   (B) isosceles
   C equilateral   D right

6. I am a quadrilateral with two pairs of congruent sides and two pairs of parallel sides. Which figure am I?

   F square   (G) rectangle
   H trapezoid   J rhombus

7. Nola makes a long-distance phone call on a pay phone. The call costs $0.85 for the first 3 minutes and $0.15 for each minute after that. Nola talks for 12 minutes. How much does the call cost?

   A $2.50   (B) $2.20   C $2.10
   D $0.90   E $2.65

8. Scientists can measure the distance to the moon by reflecting a laser beam off of its surface. The average distance to the moon is about 238,000 miles. A laser beam travels at about 186,000 miles per second. About how long does it take the beam to go to the moon and return to Earth?

   F about $1\frac{1}{4}$ sec   G about $1\frac{3}{4}$ sec

   (H) about $2\frac{1}{2}$ sec   J about $4\frac{1}{2}$ sec

   K Not Here

9. **Write About It**   Explain why you chose the answer you did in Problem 8.

   Possible answer: The trip to the moon and back is about 2 × 238,000 mi,

   or about 480,000 mi; 186,000 goes into 480,000 more than 2 times but less

   than 4 times.

Expressing Ratios

Write the correct answer.

1. Write the ratio of hearts to clubs in three different ways.

   $6 \text{ to } 8; \ 6{:}8; \ \dfrac{6}{8}$

2. Write the ratio of squares to total figures in three different ways.

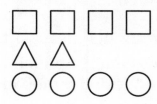

   $4 \text{ to } 10; \ 4{:}10; \ \dfrac{4}{10}$

3. Write the ratio of clubs to hearts in the figures in Problem 1 above.

   $\dfrac{8}{6}$

4. Write the ratio of triangles to circles in the figures in Problem 2 above.

   $\dfrac{2}{4}$

Choose the letter of the correct answer.

5. Which ratio is equivalent to the ratio 3 to 4?

   A 324   **B** $\dfrac{3}{4}$ C $\dfrac{4}{3}$ D $\dfrac{1}{34}$

6. Which ratio is equivalent to 7:11?

   F $\dfrac{11}{7}$ G $\dfrac{72}{11}$ H 711   **J** $\dfrac{7}{11}$

7. Which of these figures always has exactly two lines of symmetry?

   A a square
   B a rectangle
   C a circle
   D an equilateral triangle
   E Not Here

8. Ms. Stein estimates that she walks an average of 3 miles around the school every weekday. If the school year is 38 weeks long, about how far does she walk during one school year?

   F 15 mi   G 780 mi
   H 570 mi   J 114 mi
   K 1,114 mi

9. **Write About It** Explain how the ratios in Problems 1 and 2 are different.

   <u>Possible answer: The ratio in Problem 1 compares one part of a group to</u>

   <u>another part; the ratio in Problem 2 compares one part of a group to the</u>

   <u>whole group.</u>

Equivalent Ratios

Write the correct answer.

1. Write two ratios equivalent to the ratio 5:2.

   Possible answer: 10:4 and 20:8

2. Write two ratios equivalent to the ratio $\frac{1}{8}$.

   Possible answer: $\frac{2}{16}$ and $\frac{3}{24}$

3. There are 12 boys and 14 girls in Jed's classroom. Write the ratio of girls to boys.

   $$\frac{14}{12}$$

4. In Vera's class the ratio of girls to boys is 13:11. Write the ratio of girls to the whole class.

   $$\frac{13}{24}$$

Choose the letter of the correct answer.

5. Which ratio is equivalent to the ratio 6 to 14?

   A 12:21
   (B) $\frac{3}{7}$
   C 24 to 28
   D 14 to 6

6. Which ratio is equivalent to the ratio 7:2?

   F 14:1
   G 21 to 9
   H $\frac{2}{14}$
   (J) 14:4

7. The ratio of string instruments to brass instruments in the school orchestra is 1:1. Which of the following can you conclude about the orchestra?

   A It has only 2 musicians.
   B It has only 1 string musician.
   C It has only 1 brass musician.
   (D) It has equal numbers of string and brass instruments.
   E All of the Above

8. The average height between floors in the Penn Building is $10\frac{1}{2}$ feet. If the total height is 147 feet, how many floors are there in the building?

   F 8 floors   **G** 12 floors
   H 13 floors   **(J)** 14 floors
   K Not Here

9. **Write About It**   Explain why you chose the answer you did in Problem 7.

   Possible answer: The ratio 1:1 is equivalent to 2:2, 3:3, 4:4, and so on, so there are equal numbers of both types of musicians.

   _____

More About Equivalent Ratios

Write the correct answer.

1. Write the missing number in the ratio table.

Time of Snowfall	12 hr	24 hr	36 hr	48 hr
Depth of Snow	5 in.	10 in.	? in.	20 in.

_____ **15 in.** _____

2. Write the missing number in the ratio table.

Number of Pages	30	45	60	75
Time to Print	? min	9 min	12 min	15 min

_____ **6 min** _____

3. Liam has built 12 model cars and 18 model trucks. Write a ratio in three different ways comparing the number of model cars to the number of model trucks.

12:18; 12 to 18; $\frac{12}{18}$

4. Dorothy notices that the ratio of glass beads to wood beads in the necklace she is making is 3:2. Write two ratios that are equivalent to this ratio.

Possible answer: $\frac{6}{4}$ and $\frac{9}{6}$

Choose the letter of the correct answer.

5. A map scale shows that the ratio of centimeters to miles is 1 cm:10 mi. Claude measures 4 centimeters between two cities on the map. What is the actual distance between the two cities?

A 20 mi   **B** 400 mi
C 40 mi   **D** 2 mi

6. A map scale shows that the ratio of inches to kilometers is 1 in. = 60 km. The distance between two mountain peaks on the map is 7 inches. What is the actual distance between the two peaks?

F 70 km   **G** 130 km
H 600 km   **J** 420 km

7. Tom has 90 cases of cans to stack on the supermarket shelves. If he can stack 6 cases in 10 minutes, how long should it take him to stack all 90 cases?

A 10 min   **B** 90 min   **C** 60 min
D 150 min   **E** 15 min

8. Monica takes the 8:34 A.M. train. The ride is usually 40 minutes long. This morning the train is delayed by 30 minutes. What time does Monica get off the train?

F 8:44 A.M.   **G** 9:34 A.M.
H 9:39 A.M.   **J** 9:44 A.M.
K Not Here

9. Write About It Describe the method you used to solve Problem 7.

Possible answer: I made a table to find a pattern; 6 cases in 10 min means

12 in 20 min, 18 in 30 min, and so on, and 90 cases in 150 min.

Harcourt Brace School Publishers

Name _____

Ratios in Similar Figures

Write the correct answer.

1. Write *similar* or *not similar* to describe the figures.

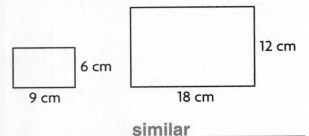

_____ **similar** _____

2. Write *similar* or *not similar* to describe the figures.

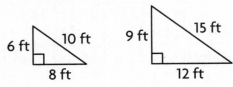

_____ **similar** _____

3. A map scale shows that 1 cm = 12 km. A park on the map is 36 kilometers long. How long will the park be on the map?

_____ **3 cm** _____

4. Dianne brings 22 ginger snaps and 16 lemon snaps to work. What is the ratio of lemon snaps to the total number of cookies?

_____ $\frac{16}{38}$ _____

Choose the letter of the correct answer.

5. A triangle has dimensions of 8 inches, 9 inches, and 10 inches. A triangle that is similar has dimensions of 24 inches and 27 inches. What is the third dimension of the similar triangle?

A 30 in.   **B** 60 in.
C 10 in.   **D** 17 in.

6. Carl can run twice as fast as his little brother. They agree to have a $\frac{1}{2}$-mile race. To make it a fair race, how much of a head start should Carl give his brother?

F $\frac{1}{8}$ mi   **G** $\frac{1}{4}$ mi   **H** $\frac{1}{3}$ mi

J $\frac{1}{2}$ mi   **K** None

7. Which ratio is equivalent to $\frac{18}{3}$?

F $\frac{21}{7}$ **G** 12:2
H 9 to 2   **J** $\frac{6}{2}$

8. Rosanna builds a tower of connecting blocks. Each layer in the tower has 4 fewer blocks than the layer below it. The bottom layer has 67 blocks in it. What is the greatest number of layers the tower can have?

F 16   **G** 17   **H** 18
J 19   **K** Not Here

9. Write About It Describe the strategy you used to solve Problem 8.

Possible answer: I made a table so I could extend the pattern from 67

down until the number of blocks in a layer became fewer than 4.

Using Pictures

As you read a problem that includes a picture, match
what you read with what you see. Look for symbols,
abbreviations, and labels that tell about the picture. Read
the following problem.

Ana made a scale model of the new
library. She found the dimensions of the
building from a copy of the architect's
plans. What length did she make
the long side of her scale model?

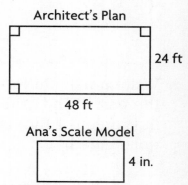

Architect's Plan

24 ft

48 ft

Ana's Scale Model

4 in.

---

1. Read the sentences in the problem.

   What picture do you look at as you read the first sentence? **Ana's Scale
   Model**

   What picture do you look at as you read the second sentence? **Architect's
   Plan**

   What picture do you look at as you read the third sentence? **both pictures**

2. Solve the problem. $\frac{24}{48}$, or $\frac{1}{2}$; $\frac{1}{2} \times \frac{4}{4} = \frac{4}{8}$; **8 in.**

3. Describe the strategy you used. **I wrote a number sentence to form an
   equivalent ratio.**

Match what you read with what you see. Solve.

4. Joao saw a picture of a house in a magazine. He made a scale drawing of the
   house, using a scale of $\frac{1}{2}$ inch = 1 foot. What are the dimensions of Joao's
   drawing?

   House length: **$31\frac{1}{2}$ in.**   House height: **10 in.**

   Length of each side of roof: **18 in.**

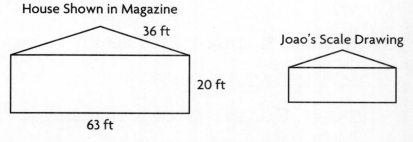

House Shown in Magazine

36 ft

20 ft

63 ft

Joao's Scale Drawing

Connecting Percents and Decimals

Write the correct answer.

1. Write a percent for
the part of the grid
that is shaded.

_____75%_____

2. Write a percent for
the part of the grid
in Problem 1 that is
not shaded.

_____25%_____

3. Out of Chester's 21 videos, 14 are
cartoons. Write a ratio comparing
the number of cartoon videos to
the total number of videos.

_____**Possible answer: 2:3**_____

4. Look at Problem 3. Write a ratio
of Chester's cartoon videos to the
videos that aren't cartoons.

_____**Possible answer: $\frac{2}{1}$**_____

Choose the letter of the correct answer.

5. A survey reports that about half of
the people surveyed would vote
for the governor in the next
election. Which is the most
reasonable percent the survey
might have found?

A 22%   B 48%
C 80%   D 99%

6. Which percent is equivalent to the
decimal 0.40?

F 4%   G 0.4%
H 40%   J 400%

7. One hundred students try out for
the play. There are parts for only
14 students in the play. Which
percent shows the part of the
students who try out but who will
not get parts in the play?

A 14%   B 76%   C 86%
D 50%   E 98%

8. A CD has 4 tracks on it. What is
the total play time of the CD?

CD Playing Time

Track	1	2	3	4
Playing Time	12 min 13 sec	6 min 54 sec	9 min 59 sec	11 min

F 42 min 50 sec G 41 min 36 sec
H 54 min 6 sec   J 40 min 6 sec

9. **Write About It** Describe the steps you took to solve Problem 7.

_____**Possible answer: I subtracted: 100 − 14 = 86 students; then I wrote a ratio:**_____

_____**86 out of 100 = 86%.**_____

Connecting Percents and Fractions

Write the correct answer.

1. Write 85% as a fraction in simplest form.

$$\frac{17}{20}$$

2. Write $\frac{4}{5}$ as a percent.

80%

3. Jackie finds that the cost of living has increased by 78% since she was born. Write 78% as a decimal.

0.78

4. Todd tests computer chips. He finds that about 4 out of every 100 chips are faulty. Write a ratio to compare the number of faulty chips to the total number of chips.

Possible answer: $\frac{4}{100}$

Choose the letter of the correct answer.

5. Which fraction is equivalent to 20%?

A $\frac{20}{10}$ **B** $\frac{2}{100}$

C $\frac{2}{10}$ **D** $\frac{2}{1,000}$

6. Which percent is equivalent to $\frac{7}{20}$?

F 35%
G 70%
H 27%
J 75%

7. Harold divides an apple pie into 8 equal slices. He then eats 6 of the slices. Which percent shows the amount of the pie he ate?

A 68%   **B** 25%   **C** 14%
D 98%   **E** 75%

8. Sheryl buys octagonal tiles for her bathroom floor. The tiles are 1 inch on each side. Which tile will she also need to buy to completely cover the floor?

F pentagons with 1-in. sides
G triangles with 1-in. sides
H squares with 1-in. sides
J squares with 2-in. sides
K Not Here

9. Write About It   Explain the strategy you used to solve Problem 8.

Possible answer: I drew a picture of the octagonal tile, and then copied it

several times and made patterns with it to see what the gaps looked like.

Benchmark Percents

Write the correct answer.

1. Which benchmark percent would you use to estimate 81%?

   10%   25%   50%   75%   100%

   _____ 75% _____

2. Which benchmark percent would you use to estimate 8%?

   10%   25%   50%   75%   100%

   _____ 10% _____

3. Mr. Boise has finished painting 75% of his house. What fraction of the house has he finished painting?

   $\frac{3}{4}$

4. Of the students on the class trip, $\frac{3}{5}$ have never visited Chicago. What percent of the students have never visited Chicago?

   _____ 60% _____

Choose the letter of the correct answer.

5. Which percent is equivalent to 0.05?

   A 20%   B 50%
   C 2%   (D) 5%

6. Which decimal is equivalent to 47%?

   (F) 0.47   G 0.047
   H 1.47   J 4.7

7. Marc has 22,553 miles on his car. He needs to take the car for a tune-up when it has 30,000 miles on it. Which of the trips below would take the car over the 30,000-mile mark?

   A two 1,600-mi trips
   B five 700-mi trips
   C a 3,000-mi trip and a 2,500-mi trip
   D twelve 350-mi trips
   (E) Not Here

8. Julia measures on her map how far she still has to drive on her trip. The distance is $4\frac{1}{2}$ in. Her map scale is 1 in. = 100 mi. If Julia's average speed is 50 miles per hour, how long will it take her to finish her trip?

   F 8 hr   G 6 hr   H 7 hr
   (J) 9 hr   K 10 hr

9. **Write About It**   Describe the steps you took to solve Problem 8.

   Possible answer: The map scale ratio is 1 in.: 100 mi, so I multiplied

   Julia's $4\frac{1}{2}$-in. measurement: $4\frac{1}{2} \times 100 = 450$ mi. Then I divided: 450 mi ÷

   50 mi per hr = 9 hr.

Percents in Circle Graphs

Write the correct answer. Use the circle graph for Problems 1 and 2.

1. Which is greater—the number of students who have pets or the number of students who do *not* have pets?

   the number who have pets

STUDENTS AND PETS

Do Not
Have Pets
45%

Have Pets
55%

2. Write a fraction to represent the students who do *not* have pets.

   Possible answer: $\frac{9}{20}$

3. Of the employees at Jones, Inc., 0.06 of them have company cars. What percent of employees have company cars?

   6%

4. One week the President's public approval rating is high: 60% of the people think he is doing a good job. What fraction of the people think the President is doing a good job?

   $\frac{3}{5}$

Choose the letter of the correct answer.

5. Which percent is equivalent to $\frac{4}{25}$?

   A 24%   **B** 100%
   C 16%   **D** 29%

6. Which percent is equivalent to 0.59?

   F 0.59%   **G** 5.9%
   H 59%   **J** 60%

7. Katie is supposed to meet Kenny at quarter to four in the afternoon. She is 35 minutes late. Kenny leaves 10 minutes before Katie arrives. What time does Kenny leave?

   A 3:15 P.M.   **B** 4:15 P.M.
   C 4:10 P.M.   **D** 4:05 P.M.
   E 4:30 P.M.

8. Ms. Saxon pays $290 each month for health insurance. Her employer pays an additional $140 each month. What is the total cost of Ms. Saxon's health insurance for the year?

   F $5,160   **G** $430
   H $3,480   **J** $1,680
   K Not Here

9. **Write About It** Explain the strategy you used to solve Problem 7.

   Possible answer: I drew a picture of a clock, counted off 35 min after

   a quarter to four, and then counted back 10 min.

Observing Relationships

When you **observe relationships**, you notice how one idea, fact, or part is connected to another idea, fact, or part. Look for similarities to decide if facts are related. Graphs are often used to show relationships of the parts to the whole. Read the following problem.

VOCABULARY

observe
relationships

In a survey, Lyn found out how many students had pets at home. She got responses from 100 students. Of the students, 40% had cats, 30% had dogs, 10% had birds, 10% had gerbils, and 10% had no pet. How can Lyn best display the data? How many students had dogs?

1. Percents and fractions show the relationship between parts and a whole.

   a. Write the percents as fractions. What is the sum of the fractions? **40% = $\frac{4}{10}$, or $\frac{2}{5}$; 30% = $\frac{3}{10}$; 10% = $\frac{1}{10}$; 10% = $\frac{1}{10}$; 10% = $\frac{1}{10}$; 1**

   b. How are the percents related to the 100 students? **The percents are the parts; the hundred students make up the whole.**

   c. Why is it that the 10% who had no pet are included in the whole? **They were part of the 100 students included in the survey.**

2. Solve the problem. **circle graph; 30 students**

3. Describe the strategy you used. **I made a circle graph.**

Underline the parts that are related to the whole. Solve.

4. Clay surveyed 200 students to find out the best date to have the school play. Of those surveyed, <u>50% wanted May 18th, 30% wanted May 19th, 10% wanted June 5th, and 10% wanted June 12th</u>. How should Clay display the data? Which date is the most popular?

   circle graph; May 18

5. Of the 50 students in a survey, <u>40% want Ed</u> for their grade representative, <u>30% want Tasha, 20% want Julio</u>, and <u>10% want Melva</u>. How can you display the data? Which student is the most popular?

   circle graph; Ed